W9-BMZ-354

THE
HOME
OFFICE

THE
HOME
OFFICE

Candace Ord Manroe

Reader's Digest

THE READER'S DIGEST ASSOCIATION, INC.
Pleasantville, New York/Montreal

A READER'S DIGEST BOOK

Prepared and produced by
Michael Friedman Publishing Group, Inc.

Copyright © 1997 by Michael Friedman Publishing Group, Inc.

All rights reserved. Unauthorized reproduction, in any manner, is prohibited.

Library of Congress Cataloging-in-Publication Data

Manroe, Candace Ord, 1954-
      The home office / Candace Ord Manroe.
         p.   cm.
      ISBN 0-89577-974-9
      1. Home offices—Management.   2. Home offices—Design.   3. Home
offices—Equipment and supplies.   I. Title
HD62.38.M36   1997
643'.58—dc21   97-9763

Reader's Digest and the Pegasus logo are registered trademarks
of The Reader's Digest Association, Inc.

Printed and bound in Great Britain by Butler & Tanner Ltd, Frome and London

To my children
Meagan, Drew, and Sam

TABLE OF CONTENTS

INTRODUCTION

PEOPLE WHO HAVE A HOME OFFICE SHARE A SECRET: THEY KNOW THE PLEASURE OF ROLLING OUT OF BED, GETTING A CUP OF COFFEE, AND DIVING RIGHT INTO WORK WITHOUT FUSSING WITH MAKEUP or finding a clean shirt. Furthermore, they have a great advantage over those who travel miles to work, whether by car, by bus, or by train. They don't waste time commuting, nor do they have to deal with delays, crowded trains, and traffic jams. Some commuters can lose more than two hours every day in the rat race. Those who don't have to commute can claim that time for themselves.

A home office is useful even if it's used only part-time. Those who are swamped at work because there isn't enough time in the day to catch up or those who are very ambitious and want to get ahead don't have to stay in a deserted office building late at night. And for those who enjoy working hard at a hobby, a home office provides an organized, functional space in which to get a project done.

For almost all occupations, ever-changing, ever-improving technology has made it increasingly easier to work at home. The personal computer and other technological advances of the past decade, such as the fax machine and the modem, are changing not only how people communicate but how they live. These changes have been pivotal in making the home office the newest essential room in the home.

This book will teach you how to successfully create an office in your home. Tips are included throughout to help you make decisions about everything from lighting to upholstery options. You will learn to develop a space plan and find the layout that works best for you.

Chapter 1 will challenge you to identify your needs and preferences and will offer solutions for meeting them. You may be fortunate enough to have an entire room in your home to devote to an office, or you may have to be more inventive, and set up shop in a nook or cranny somewhere in your home. Either way, chapter 2 will help you find the best location in your home for your office.

The most fun you'll have when creating a home office is personalizing it. When it's time to undertake the decorating process, be sure to map out a detailed budget so you'll know exactly how much work you can do on your office space before you get started. Chapter 3 will show you what wall and window treatments, fabrics, floorings, and more will make your home office a desirable work space.

In chapter 4, you will learn how to plan a layout and choose furniture that will make your office both functional and beautiful. Finally, chapter 5 will address your equipment needs. Don't forget to establish a budget for furniture and equipment.

NOTE: Before you embark on your home office venture, be sure to check your local zoning laws. Some communities have laws restricting certain types of businesses from operating in residential neighborhoods.

CHAPTER ONE

AN OFFICE FOR EVERY PURPOSE

Technology is one of the most important influences behind the emergence of the home office. But it's not just the computer-minded who require these spaces. Anyone—even a homeowner who has no interest in or need for office equipment but who still appreciates a quiet spot just for taking care of household accounts—can benefit from an office in the home.

ALL KINDS OF OFFICES

Many activities, from sewing and carpentry to financial planning and desktop publishing, are best pursued in a specially designed environment. Depending on what you want to accomplish and how much time you will spend in your office, you can determine which type of home office is best suited to you. Below are some variations.

■ *The Full-time Workplace*

Thanks to technology, more and more people are discovering how thoroughly and conveniently they can get the job done without ever leaving their homes. Employers also appreciate this new concept of satellite home offices because it means that they can keep a lid on expenses by reducing overhead. In this case, the home office isn't a convenience for those times when it's necessary to bring work home but an essential space for working full-time at home.

If you have a family, having a full-time workplace in the home means that one parent will be available to children in emergencies. When the school nurse calls, for example, you can easily pick up a child from school. Commuting time and costs are also eliminated when

This office set up in the corner of a living room is used as a full-time work space. Because the office faces away from the room, it is easier to focus on work and ignore distractions.

your home office is your full-time office. And unless you'll see clients in your home office, think of all the money you'll save on dry cleaning and all the wasted time and aggravation you'll avoid by not rushing to get to the office.

If the home office is to function as a full-time workplace within your home, it needs to be treated as such. Privacy is essential for ensuring professionalism on business phone calls and during meetings and for concentrating on the tasks at hand. Consider how you can make the space quieter. Depending on the scale of renovations needed to create your home office, this could entail installing new walls and a door or just adding some sound-absorbing material.

Although the full-time office doesn't have to be huge, it should be adequately large to accommodate the furnishings,

When planning your office, be sure to give attention to the aesthetics of the space. An environment that is pleasing to you will improve your performance. Here, an antique table serves as a desk in the back of a lushly decorated living room.

ABOVE: An after-hours office can be easily set up in any area of your home—using existing furniture. Here, an antique desk is tucked into in a niche in the living room.

OPPOSITE TOP: A home office is the perfect location for a designer to finish leftover projects.

OPPOSITE BOTTOM: A full-time space is needed to accommodate this crafter's hobby. Flower arrangements are hung from the ceiling, creating both a great storage solution and a decorative element. Customized built-in shelving displays the finished arrangements.

equipment, and work space necessary for doing the job. Because an entire workday will be spent here, construction of the environment should also take into consideration such things as views, exposures, and decorating aesthetics. Furnishings should not only look good but feel good. For example, your desk chair should conform to the shape of your body to prevent the tiredness and soreness that may occur if you spend the day in an uncomfortable chair. (See The Desk Chair on page 102 for more information.)

■ *The After-hours Office*

For the workaholic, a home office equipped with a computer means a substantially lighter stack of work being transported home. The worker who can't call it a day at five o'clock can easily bring home a project on a diskette and continue working into the night.

A home office used for taking care of spillover work doesn't require as much emphasis on views (most of the hours spent here will be after dark, anyway), decoration (with less time spent here, this won't become an issue), or space (bulky, space-guzzling office equipment can be used the next day at the company). While an entire room may be necessary for a full-time home office, an after-hours auxiliary office can be comfortably squeezed into a small space if necessary. Privacy isn't as crucial to this type of home office either, since most of

your phone calls will be made during regular working hours. However, remember that you will still require a certain amount of privacy to get your work done properly.

▪ *A Craft or Hobby Station*

Crafters and hobbyists know what a pleasure it is to have a place to call their own, in which they can set up a pottery wheel or spread out the fabric pieces needed for a quilting project. A home office can provide the perfect place to pursue a hobby or run a successful crafting business.

Technology has created an outlet from which everyone can benefit and has provided the opportunity to create a home office for occupations that haven't traditionally needed one. Consider the serious chef whose collection of recipes and cookbooks can now be cataloged on the computer for quick retrieval. Placing an office area somewhere close to the kitchen, or even within the kitchen in the form of a built-in desk or work booth, or in a butler's pantry would be the ideal.

In theory, the hobby office can co-exist alongside other functions in a single room, but it typically requires more customization than some of the other types of home offices. A thorough appraisal of

OPPOSITE: In a woodworker's garage "office," ample cabinets were built to house supplies. A shelf keeps screwdrivers, chisels, and other tools readily available. BELOW: All you may need to get monthly household finances in order is a niche in the kitchen. A bulletin board holds photos and momentos.

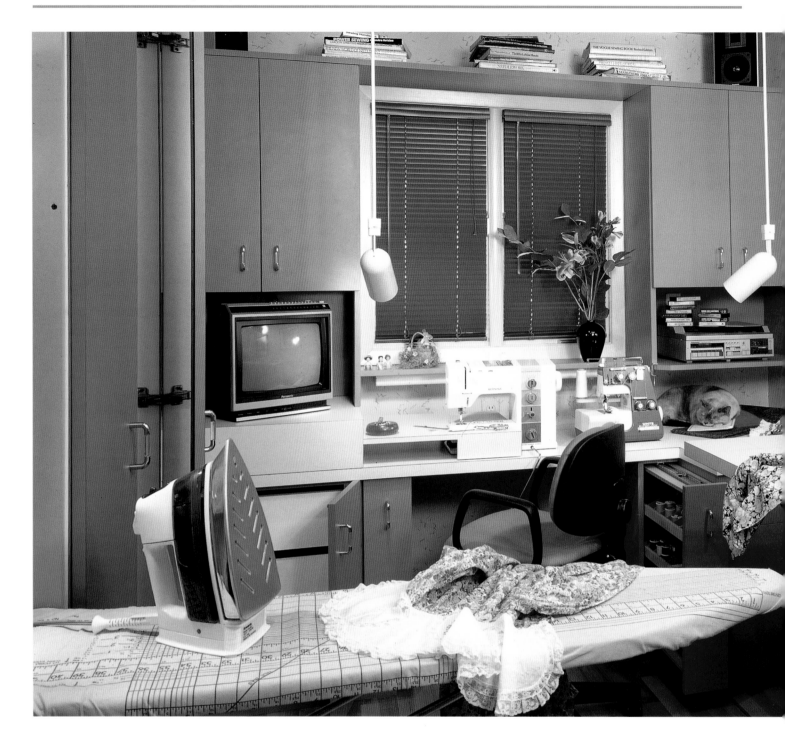

what's necessary to outfit a well-designed hobby office is recommended before setting up this space in a shared area. For example, a dressmaker needs a hobby office with space for a sewing machine, a thread and tool organizer, and a long, wide table. Having a safe, out-of-the-way space for needles, scissors, shears, and seam rippers is a good idea if you have small children. If collections of fabrics and threads are a part of your hobby, easy-to-view storage is also necessary. This may entail finding a private room, however, as the materials on display may take away from the other purpose of the room.

■ Household Management

If you are in charge of running the household, you would probably like

on a shelf and brought to the kitchen table when it was bill-paying time. Now families can plan their budgets and do their taxes electronically. All that is needed is the right software, a laptop or a desktop computer, and a printer. (Although the computer neatly stores your vital household files in its memory, it is advisable to keep files of printouts and receipts nearby.)

If you are a novice at computing, you may have a bit of trouble at first. But with a little experience, you will appreciate the ease with which you can organize your finances, figure out what you owe in taxes, and plan a month of meals. These days there's almost no limit to what you can do on the computer. You can track the schedule of each member of your family, plan a vacation, and do research for a high school history paper.

You probably won't use your household office every day or even every week. Thus, you will probably put your desk, files, and any electronic wizardry in the bedroom or in a nook near the kitchen, as these rooms usually have an informal atmosphere. The most important consideration you'll have is to make the office blend in with the room's decor.

A PLANNING CHECKLIST

Whether you're planning your office yourself or working with a designer or an architect, take time to evaluate your needs, and don't forget to look closely at your preferences. Having what you need and what you like in your home office

to have an organized place to which you can escape from the clamor of the house, a place where you can balance the checkbook or figure out the family budget. A desk and a filing cabinet may be all you need—unless you want to work electronically.

Before the personal computer existed, families planned budgets using a household ledger. It was stored in a drawer or

A dressmaker's office decorated in shades of dusty rose is as functional as it is appealing. One workstation has a desk with two sewing machines and another has a table large enough to spread out yards of fabric. The ironing board is set up when needed and hidden behind a closet door when not in use. A television and a stereo system help to make working more enjoyable.

will ensure that your space is both functional and pleasurable. The answers you give to the questions below will help you with planning and prevent costly mistakes.

When planning your office space, try to include a comfortable spot to rest. This office features a plush armchair and a table stacked with books and magazines.

▪ *Evaluating Your Needs*

Whether your new office will be an at-home location for pursuing full-time employment or will be used on a more casual basis will make a huge difference in how you approach its design. First identify which type of office it will be, then ask yourself the following questions.

1) HOW MUCH TIME WILL YOU BE SPENDING IN YOUR HOME OFFICE?

The more time you will spend in your office each week, the more important it is to design a space that's eminently comfortable, not merely functional. If you immediately retreat to your home office or hobby station as soon as you come home from work, the work space will assume a greater importance for you than it would for someone spending fewer hours in it.

If weeks will go by between visits to your home office, it's not necessary to make it spacious or to decorate it with expensive furniture. Be honest about how much time you'll be spending in this space and you'll save yourself time and money.

2) WHAT TASKS WILL YOU DO HERE?

Using books and periodicals for research, for example, requires room to spread out, as do any number of other activities conducted in a home office. Jobs that

ABOVE: Plants help make you feel at home in your office. Before you make any purchases, be sure to do a little research. Some plants thrive in bright light; others prefer indirect light.

OPPOSITE: This his-and-hers home office is set up in a hallway. Both laptop computers are hooked into one printer, saving space and money.

require ample elbowroom are best performed at a work area larger than a desk—either a conference table or a long island-style or built-in workstation. If you work on a computer and also write with pen and paper, you will need a space for both.

Determine which tasks will be occupying most of your time, then plan an office that prioritizes these pursuits above others.

3) WHAT EQUIPMENT AND FURNITURE IS ESSENTIAL? Imagine yourself working in your home office. This will help you figure out what kind of equipment you'll need. For example, if your home office will be devoted primarily to running the household, it makes sense to stock it with an easy-to-use calculator that's always ready to serve. If you are scrupulous about making copies of all your legal documents, tax records, and other

HELPFUL HINT
If you will be using equipment in your office that uses a lot of electricity, consider having a separate circuit added to your home's wiring. This will help you avoid constantly blowing fuses and losing computer files because of power overloads.

BELOW: An artist requires a good balance of natural and artificial light. To supplement the large windows, track lighting provides a sense of warmth to this space while an overhead fluorescent fixture provides direct lighting for the task at hand.

important papers, or if your occupation requires you to make copies of everything (if you're a lawyer or a researcher, for example), it may be worthwhile, in terms of both time and money, for you to outfit your home office with a personal copy machine.

One of the most important considerations you'll have in making your home office a pleasant place to work is to decide what pieces of furniture you'll need. Some furniture is necessary to house the equipment you require; other pieces may not be essential at all but can make life easier and more pleasant. For example, you may not need a sofa or loveseat in your home office, but this piece of furniture might be helpful to you when you need to take a break but don't want to leave your office. Also, if you will be conducting meetings in the

office, you should have furniture to seat visitors comfortably.

Prioritize by putting the equipment and furnishings you absolutely need at the top of your list and making luxuries secondary. The latter are the appealing and useful, but nonessential items that you may be able to add later on (see Extras on page 34). You may wish to buy furniture in stages, purchasing the most essential items first to make the expenditure more affordable. By thinking ahead, you'll be able to make wise, quick decisions when it's time to spend money.

4) HOW MANY SQUARE FEET DO YOU NEED?

Many would love a spacious home office, with room to store old files, finished projects, or a book collection, or one large enough in which to lounge comfortably when a break is necessary. This, however, is a luxury for most people. After determining which tasks you must perform in the office and the equipment and furniture you require, decide how much space is absolutely necessary. You may find that it is far less than you had imagined. This opens up the possibility of the office being located in a corner of a

An expanse of windows provides a glorious source of light in this space. But if you will be easily distracted by the view or want to control the amount of sunlight in the room, invest in unobtrusive blinds that can be pulled down when need be.

room or even in a closet that you had not considered before. You will also be able to rule out those spaces that are too small for your purposes.

5) WILL YOU BE RECEIVING CLIENTS OR SUPPLIERS IN THE OFFICE OR USING IT AS A PRIVATE SPACE? If clients, suppliers, or coworkers will be meeting with you in your home office, you may want to locate the space in an area of the home with direct access to the outdoors. A private entry to the office is not only more convenient, it's more professional than having your guests parade through a family room scattered with children's toys or the Sunday newspaper.

If you have to hold meetings in your home office, privacy is a necessity. The office should be quiet and visually set apart from the rest of the home, either as a private room of its own or as an area that can be closed off if needed.

ABOVE: A small workstation constructed in the same wood as the existing kitchen cabinets provides a good space to schedule doctor's appointments and soccer games for a family. The unit has been designed so that when it's not in use, a panel closes off the desk.

LEFT: If you are planning to have clients in your office, you'll want the space to be impressive. In this case, the unusual shape of the room is emphasized with long brick walls. An oversize marble desk/conference table dominates the center of the room, while softer elements—stuffed chairs, paintings, and plants—are arranged along the opposite walls.

ABOVE: Chinese red paint and upholstered furniture and curtains in the same tropical flower print jazz up this living room office.

OPPOSITE: Sometimes the best environment in which to work is one that suggests serenity and relaxation. Working in this space may feel more like sitting down to tea.

■ *Evaluating Your Preferences*

After you've determined your fundamental needs for creating a successful office environment at home, it is time to evaluate your preferences. Preferences are usually more idiosyncratic in nature than needs. When evaluating your preferences, be sure to take into account your own habits, strengths, and weaknesses. Ask yourself the following questions.

1) WOULD YOU LIKE A PLAIN ENVIRONMENT OR A MORE VISUALLY LIVELY SPACE IN WHICH TO WORK?

Not everyone thrives in an environment alive with visual stimulation—lively rhythms in patterns, colors, and objects. Some require a simpler environment to really concentrate and keep thoughts as uncluttered as the surrounding walls. The colorful, highly charged family room that you love spending time in with friends may not be the ideal workplace for you, despite its appeal. Conversely, the soft palette of the bedroom, which makes for soothing sleep, may not be bold enough to keep you alert. Examine your personality honestly before deciding what your office space should look like.

2) DO YOU NEED TOTAL PRIVACY TO WORK WELL, OR IS YOUR PERFORMANCE ENHANCED BY A SENSE OF CONNECTEDNESS TO OTHERS?

A home office does not necessarily have to be separated from the rest of the house to allow you to function efficiently. Some may feel too isolated working on the third floor in a secluded attic-turned-office. A guest bedroom on the main floor of the home or even a section of a family room or the kitchen could be a much better choice.

On the other hand, those with a low tolerance for noise may find the more isolated home office better suited to them. The conversion of a basement, an attic, or even a garage, where the office is cut off from activity in the home, could be the ideal space. Decide

OPPOSITE: With an expanse of windows that looks out upon the ocean, little decoration is needed in this office. The room's muted palette makes the most of the glorious view.

whether you prefer connectedness or isolation when choosing a space for your home office.

3) Do Your Surroundings Influence How Well You Concentrate?

For most people, a window is a vital connection to the world, without which they feel claustrophobic and uncomfortable. If you're one of these people, make a priority of finding a location with a window for your workstation.

Be honest with yourself, however. If a window will encourage you to daydream, make sure your desk does not face a window or that the office is in a windowless room or space. Otherwise, you may find you get very little done.

4) What Color Schemes Would Work Best in Your Home Office?

Just as a view of the outdoors can influence your work, so can the colors used to decorate the space. In general, color has a definite psychological impact on mood, and it will influence the mood of your office as well. So whether you decorate the space from scratch or decide to share space in an existing decor, consider carefully the colors with which you surround yourself. If a room that is

a good candidate for sharing functions has a color scheme that is too somber or too bright, for example, you may have to redecorate—or reconsider.

TAKING THE NEXT STEP

With your needs and preferences mapped out, you should have a firm grasp on what will constitute your home office. The next step is to take a tour of your home and look objectively at each room as a potential location to set up shop. Remember, closets, garages, and unfinished attics or basements are possible spaces for conversion to an office.

Be on the lookout for spaces that can satisfy your needs with little or no alteration: spaces that have ample windows (if a view of the outdoors is desirable), an appropriate color scheme, adequate wall and floor space, a private entry (if that is one of your requirements), adequate isolation from or integration into the rest of the home, and other features brought to your attention in the planning checklist. You may be surprised at the number of options you have.

EXTRAS

Once you've determined which items you must have in your office space, decide which special "extras" you'd like to include. Extras are not necessarily expensive, but they can eat up precious space. Be sure that you have the floor space or the shelf or cabinet space needed to accommodate them. Here are just a few of the extras you may want to have:

RADIO OR SOUND SYSTEM

Whether you play classical or jazz to soothe you as you work, or rock with a fast beat to keep you working, music can improve your performance. A Walkman easily blocks out background noise, enhancing your ability to concentrate. For convenience, you may wish to store a second set of tapes and compact discs in your office.

TELEVISION/VCR

If you want to be on top of world events, you can keep a small TV in your home office or in close proximity to your work space. You might also want a TV around just to take a five-minute break to catch up on your favorite soap. And, if your work requires occasional video research, it's a good idea to have a VCR handy. You might also be inspired to pop in an exercise tape on a break.

SMALL REFRIGERATOR

This appliance will save you trips to the kitchen. Stock your refrigerator with plenty of juices, soda, water, and snacks—whatever will keep you going.

MICROWAVE

Microwavable dishes and snacks such as popcorn makes a great treat when you're burning the midnight oil. Having a microwave close by means not having to journey to the kitchen and wait there while it runs. You'll also know when it's time to rotate the package and when it's done.

EXERCISE MACHINE

A 10- or 15-minute workout on an exercise bike, treadmill, or Stairmaster will help you return to your work refreshed.

HOUSEPLANTS

Whether large or small, plants grown in containers bring nature indoors (especially if you have small, or no, windows) and provide a calming influence. A grow light can be used to improve existing light.

ART, ANTIQUES, AND OBJETS D'ART

These items personalize a home office, making it truly yours. Although limited space means you won't be able to display everything at once, you can change the exhibit every so often. In addition, be sure to leave some room for other momentos.

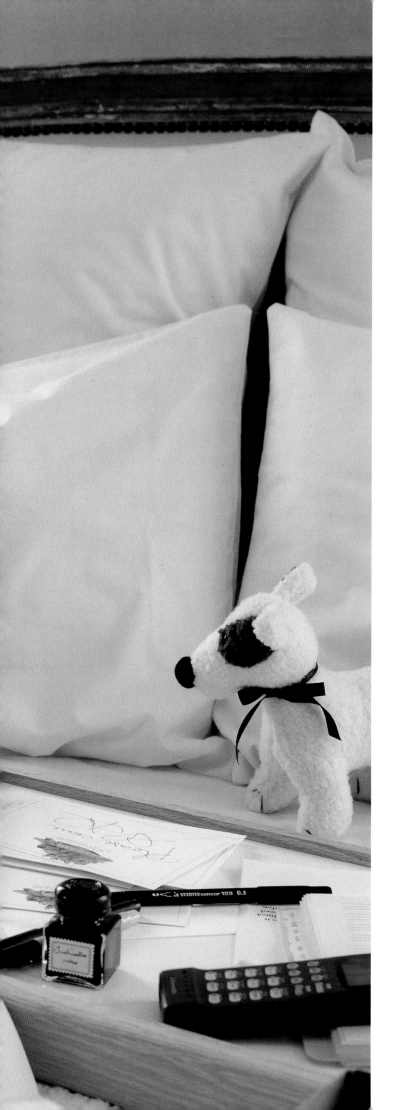

CHAPTER TWO

FINDING ROOM

After you've decided what kind of office works for you, it's time to find a place in your home to set up shop. Maybe you will find that you have a full room to devote to office use, or maybe you'll need to be more creative, sharing space or setting up in a nook or cranny of your home. This chapter will help you find the best location.

A ROOM OF ONE'S OWN

Not every home or apartment has extra rooms available for office use, but chances are, your living quarters offer more space than you think. Creating an office in your home could mean making architectural changes, such as knocking down or putting up walls, but it could be as easy as altering the space's present function and filling it with your office equipment and furniture.

The following room-by-room guide will help you decide whether using a whole room as your home office is the right solution for you. The information on climate, wiring, lighting, and decorating will help you avoid making costly mistakes.

■ *The Extra Bedroom*

One of the best locations for a home office is the extra bedroom. Unless you have overnight guests on a regular basis, there's little reason to waste this precious square footage on a bedroom. And the guest-bedroom-turned-office can still accommodate an occasional visitor. Thus, when considering furniture and equipment for your office (see chapters 4 and 5), plan to install a sofa that has a pull-out bed or other seating that easily converts into a bed, such as a futon. Dressers or chests of drawers can act as multipurpose furnishings, providing guests with a place to keep their clothes and serving as another surface on which to put equipment and papers.

Some extra bedrooms are set apart from the main public areas of the home.

Here, a spare bedroom has been converted into an artist's studio. Collectibles line the shelves and serve as inspiration for the artist's own works. A canvas sheet protects the floor from spills and splatters.

For one who loves privacy and works best in seclusion, this can be ideal. But if you will be meeting with clients or customers in your home office, such a room will not provide you with a separate entrance to the office. You may not mind parading visitors through the main body of your home, into the private sleeping wing—but then again, depending on your housekeeping standards, you may.

Climate control, wiring, and lighting are not issues when you consider this kind of conversion. As an integral part of the family living space, the extra bedroom is already on the home's heating, cooling, and wiring systems.

Decorating options for the guest bedroom are boundless. A relatively nonpublic spot in your home, this room could be a great place in which to experiment with a new decorative paint treatment you've been dying to try out or to see how much you like vinyl tile. If you're a crafter, you can use your office as a gallery of your work, both showing off your creations and decorating your space at the same time. Check the list of decorating ideas on page 48 for inspiration.

■ *Lofts*

In newer homes with open floor plans, a loft is a common feature. This space can be used for a number of functions: a family room or an informal living room, a playroom with a pool table, or a study with built-in bookshelves and a reading area. Why not make it your home office?

This loft space has a streamlined desk that fits right up against the railing. A chair, borrowed from another room, was made more comfortable with pillows. As a rule, a loft office is a semi-private place that works well for some offices, but not for others.

HELPFUL HINT
Hanging a curtain, "wall" of beads, or tapestry over the opening of your loft space can help you block out distractions. You may also try using a dressing or shoji screen to add a decorative touch.

In this attic space, shelves were built in around large windows to accommodate an extensive book collection. Wall sconces were added above the windows to supplement natural light.

Like the guest room, the loft space will already be running on the home's existing electrical wiring and heating and cooling systems and will very likely already be decorated, so you will have fewer issues to face in this conversion than you would with an unfinished attic or basement space. The office loft space has its drawbacks, though. The openness of the loft will leave you aware of the rest of the goings-on in the house, so if you are easily distracted, this space will not be appropriate for you. On the other hand, if you want a sense of community, the loft space may be your best bet.

■ *Attics and Basements*

Attics and basements are often overlooked as possible choices for general living spaces because they are often dim, damp, drafty, and good only for storage purposes. But take another look. Your attic or basement has the potential to be the ideal spot for your new home office.

Both rooms have special characteristics that make them good options. For example, if you're looking to be set apart from the rest of the home, both the attic and the basement, as the uppermost and lowest areas of the home, are hard-to-beat locations. With its sloping roofline and under-the-eaves nooks typical in most house styles, the attic possesses some of the most charming architecture in the home. The basement usually has a separate entrance. And because both of these areas are typically unfinished, they

This basement home office is flexible, functional, and comfortable. The conference area of the home office here has been optimally designed to use all available light. A halogen-bounce light treatment doubles the light from the lamp alone. The walls were sponge-painted to look sunsplashed.

HELPFUL HINT
A strategically placed dehumidifier will drastically cut down the humidity in your basement. You'll be amazed at the difference.

provide a blank canvas for creativity in your decorating scheme.

Still, for all their potential, there are some pitfalls you should be aware of before starting an attic or basement conversion. Among these are climate control, wiring, and lighting issues. Suggestions for handling these problems in both rooms are provided below.

BASEMENTS

Because of their subterranean location, basements tend to be very humid. This humidity can pose a problem for a home office, warping and rotting furnishings in the most severe cases. But don't rule out the basement because of its humidity. Consider adding wall and flooring

surfaces that repel moisture. Choose harder, less porous flooring materials, such as stone or tile, instead of wall-to-wall carpeting, which will only absorb moisture and create problems with mildew and odor.

Seepage—rainwater leaking into the basement through openings in the walls and floor—is a much bigger problem than basement humidity. Be sure to consult with a professional contractor to find out whether the moisture in your basement is normal or is caused by seepage before you spend any time or money on converting your basement. There is no easy or inexpensive way to correct this structural problem. If your basement suffers from seepage, leave your plans to convert that space into your home office behind you.

Basements also have a tendency to be drafty. While pleasingly cool in the hot summer months, they can be unpleasantly cold in winter. Insulation is the best way to combat drafts. When finishing a basement, add insulation before installing wall treatments. Another way to raise the air temperature of your basement is to invest in a couple of portable heaters. (Be especially cautious if you employ these, as they can be safety hazards if left on unattended.)

Using warm-colored and textured textiles will also offset the chill of the basement home office. An area rug placed over hard, nonporous flooring will not only make the basement office softer and pleasant, it will add a sense of warmth to the space. Furnishings that

ESCAPING THE BLAND BOX BEDROOM

In her suburban home, Deb Riha wanted a special space for her home office. She planned to include some of the features of a traditional office, such as a desk and a computer, but wanted the overall feel of the space to be anything but traditional.

Her home's only available room, the upstairs guest bedroom, lacked the kind of character and warmth she believed was essential for such a retreat. The bedroom was a white box devoid of architectural character. But Deb was hopeful.

Before personalizing the space with accessories and art, she addressed the architectural shell itself. Her goal: to create visual interest where there was none—without a major expenditure. Her solution required nothing more than a game

plan, paint, some narrow masking tape, and some strips of molding.

First she painted the room from ceiling to floor with two coats of pale green paint. Then she sectioned off the lower portion of the wall at chair-rail height. After the paint was completely dry, she applied vertical stripes of the narrow tape from the chair-rail height to the floor and painted this lower portion of the wall a crisp white. When the white paint dried, she carefully removed the tape, revealing pale green vertical pinstripes at regular intervals. She then added molding to the wall at the chair-rail height. The result is a convincing wainscoting that's more interesting than the real thing—and much less expensive.

ABOVE and TOP: Riha created a faux wainscot on the walls by painting over strips of narrow tape.

HELPFUL HINT
An attic needs to be properly ventilated to protect insulation from condensation. Check to see that your attic has a roof vent, which allows moisture to escape from insulated areas.

To break up the hard masonry background in this basement office, an artistic arrangement of twigs in a decorative vase, framed pictures leaning against the wall, and furniture in warm tones were included in the design. An area rug also helps soften the space.

will maximize the perceived warmth of the space include those that are upholstered in "warm" fabrics, such as wools or wool blends. (For information on various fabrics, see the chart on page 98.)

If the basement is very cold, you may have to revamp your home's heating system to provide a greater concentration of heat in the basement. This is likely to cost more money and take more time than you are willing to spend. If you don't think the noninvasive measures discussed here will be effective in keeping your basement office warm and comfortable, consider locating your office in another room.

Chances are, your basement is already equipped with an overhead lighting fixture. If not, a qualified electrician can easily install one by running wiring from the floor above. The electrician will also have to install the electrical outlets that you will need if your office equipment requires electricity to run.

You may also need an extra circuit if the equipment you will be using requires large amounts of electricity. (Do not attempt to undertake any of these projects yourself unless you are a licensed electrician.)

Table and floor lamps provide softer, more direct lighting to your work space. They can also be used as a decorative touch. The ideal solution for lighting your basement is to employ a combination of both.

ATTICS

The climate conditions of attics and basements are the opposite of each other. The uppermost space in the home, the attic is typically much warmer than the other rooms are, especially if it has been insulated. But the attic's climate problems can be solved as easily as the basement's.

Air-conditioning and heating are features most attics lack. Before either one is added, the attic should be properly insulated. Perhaps the only insulation that exists in your attic is from the ceiling of the story below. Additional insulation needs to be added at the roofline between the rafters. A sheet of plastic should then be stretched as a vapor barrier between the insulation and the drywall.

Most do-it-yourselfers will find hanging rolls of insulation or blowing in insulation an easy weekend project. Or you can find a professional by getting recommendations from knowledgeable friends or looking in the Yellow Pages under the Insulation Contractors listing.

Once the attic is properly insulated, you can decide which kind of heating and cooling systems to use. A home's existing central heat/air-conditioning system can be routed to the attic by running ducts there. Or it may be more efficient to add a second air-conditioning/heating source just for the attic. Depending upon the size of the area, nothing more

than a window air-conditioning unit and a space heater may be needed to keep the temperature in the attic office pleasant year-round.

As with the basement, the perceived climate of the attic is influenced by its flooring. Carpeting heightens the sense of warmth while buffering sounds from the floor below. To combat the heat you may encounter in the attic space, a cooler flooring material can be installed. Vinyl tiles are a compromise, as they offer both the cool reflectiveness of harder ceramic tiles or stone and the cushioning sound insulation of a softer textile flooring.

Think twice before planning to bathe your attic office in natural light and fresh air with new windows. Try, instead, to enlarge existing ones. Another way to increase the natural light is to add skylights. These will infuse the space with natural overhead light.

As for the basement, make sure to call a qualified electrician to wire your

> **HELPFUL HINT**
> If you are thinking of installing skylights in your attic, be sure to go through a reputable manufacturer. Ask trusted friends who have had success with a contractor. Faulty or poorly installed skylights can let in unwanted moisture and cause your roof to leak.

An attic is a good choice for any office, although the slant of the roofline can make the space seem cramped. To solve the problem in this architect's office, skylights were added and the walls and ceiling were painted white. White wall-to-wall carpeting was also installed to visually enlarge the space.

attic. Existing wiring may not meet current codes and may therefore be dangerous, especially in older homes. Let an expert make that determination.

▤ *Garages*

Converting a garage into a home office space will present you with many of the same issues as converting the basement or attic. An attached garage offers you the convenience of staying close to your household's doings while being separate at the same time.

Detached garages provide optimum privacy, but working there may make you feel somewhat isolated. You should also take into consideration that you will be out of earshot of the kids and the doorbell. Because this type of garage is independent of the house, you have a little more leeway in transforming it.

Be careful when converting garage space, as the remodeling may lessen the architectural integrity of the house. Substituting outside garage doors with permanent architectural features, such as an entry door, and adding additional windows or skylights may be part of your plan, but be careful to preserve your home's architectural style. A driveway that terminates at a big plate glass window is probably not the right solution if you own an old Victorian house, for example. Integrity should be maintained for aesthetic reasons—and because a change could affect the house's resale value.

You may also want to renovate the breezeway, hallway, or other area where the garage connects to the rest of the

OPPOSITE: Some urban apartments were once commercial spaces. Adding skylights in this top-floor loft bathes the space in natural light and atmosphere. The flue pipe that runs up from the building's wood-burning stove is a source of warmth.

BELOW: Converting a garage into office space can provide ample work space. Here, there is room for several workstations, an oversize shelving unit, and several filing cabinets.

GIVE STYLE TO A PLAIN ROOM

If a room is boxy and plain, there are a range of face-lift treatments that will spruce it up. Chapter three describes many of the following approaches in further detail.

- ■ trompe l'oeil
- ■ faux finishes
- ■ textured or patterned wall coverings
- ■ stenciling
- ■ sponge painting
- ■ mosaic designs
- ■ fabrics

- ■ coffered ceilings
- ■ wainscoting
- ■ decorative lamps, wall sconces, torchères
- ■ carpeting
- ■ decorative moldings
- ■ vinyl floor coverings
- ■ faux wood flooring

house to provide a better transition from room to room. In some homes, the garage is connected to the kitchen or basement. If this is the case, you may wish to create a separate entry for your new office in order to welcome visitors more comfortably.

As in attic and basement conversions, a garage conversion requires that you tackle drywalling, install flooring and additional wiring (having outlets and overhead wires installed where you want them), along with lighting, and heating and cooling systems.

MULTIPURPOSE ROOMS

In your quest to create an office space in your home, you may find that you don't have an extra room to devote to office use. But with a little ingenuity, you can find a suitable place. Most any room in your home can be made to serve more than one function. A bedroom's primary function is sleeping quarters, but that doesn't mean it can't also be outfitted with a computer or a sewing center. And although a dining room's raison d'être is for consuming meals, the dining table can serve another practical function.

A careful investigation of your home may reveal viable areas for an office that you never even considered. Walk through the home, room by room, and look inside the closets. Second-floor stairway landings, under-the-stairs niches, butler's pantries (in older homes), and walk-in closets are only some of the possibilities you may not have previously considered for an office space. The dining room, bedroom, living or family room, and kitchens are others.

■ *The Dining Room*

Although it may at first seem unlikely, the dining room, a room designed for formal gatherings and family meals, is a good place to set up your office. The reason for this is simple: the single requisite furnishing in the dining room—the table—is also essential to the home office. A large table, such as you would find in a dining room, allows you

ABOVE: This apartment achieves multipurpose efficiency with grace. A built-in workstation has been included in the sleeping area, helping to utilize every inch of available space.

LEFT: The decor of this home was not compromised when a mini-office was installed. By using traditional furnishings, the desk area blends in with the rest of the house.

to spread out your papers or hobby materials. A sideboard stores not only table linens and silverware but a cache of pencils, paper clips, stapler, and other needed office items.

If you have just moved into your home and have not furnished your dining room yet, you have the flexibility to choose furniture with the room's dual purpose in mind. The straight-back chair adequate for dining may cause back strain when used for hours as a desk chair (see The Desk Chair on page 102). Upholstered dining chairs are better for a dining room serving both office and dining functions. A fine wood tabletop will be prone to nicks and scratches from your equipment as well as from more frequent wear and tear. Consider a more resilient material for your dining room furniture, or invest in an acrylic or glass covering for your tabletop to protect the finish.

Chances are, though, that your furniture is already purchased and you're not willing to change it at this point. You can have a piece of glass or acrylic custom-cut (and shaped) to your table. If you are not willing to change the surface of your dining room table, visit an office supply store. Here, you will find inexpensive cardboard desk blotters with which you can cover your table. Or you can collapse cardboard boxes and cover the surface of your table with the flattened pieces. They can be easily stored in a closet when they're not in use.

Office equipment should be portable so as not to distract from the dining room's original function. A laptop computer that can be set up on the dining table during "office hours," then tucked out of sight during dinnertime, is preferable to a full-size computer or a typewriter that must remain in place all the time. Using a cordless or cellular telephone is better than having a telephone permanently in the dining room.

■ The Bedroom

For some, the bedroom may be the only available space in which to set up a home office. Although the bedroom is usually perceived as a private refuge

BELOW LEFT: A bedroom is a convenient location for an office. In this large room, a desk was easily built in beneath a bank of windows. Skylights overhead bring in more natural light, making this a bright and airy work space.
BELOW RIGHT: Loft beds are an efficient use of space. Here, a work space has been neatly tucked under the bed.

from the rest of the world, you can still accommodate a home office here. Manufacturers are now producing furniture pieces that serve a particular function but have the appearance of serving another. When furnishing your home office, look for computer stations that can be disguised as elegant-looking armoires. When the home office is in use, the doors of the piece are opened and the keyboard, printer, and monitor can be pulled out. When it's time for bed, just close the home office away in its neat little package.

▣ *The Living Room or Family Room*

What the home office in the living or family room may lack in privacy is more than compensated for in convenience. And because the family spends most of their time here, it is easy to get access to the necessary papers and files without leaving children unattended. Simple tasks can even be sandwiched in during television commercial breaks. And like the bedroom office, an office in these rooms can be tucked into an armoire.

Comfortable chairs, an area rug, and furniture with curving lines soften the boxiness of this sleek, urban living room.

HELPFUL HINT
You can custom build a workstation in a closet to maximize the amount of space available to you. Portable, stackable plastic organizers configured to your specific needs will also help you utilize every possible square inch of space.

RIGHT: This kitchen office is a convenient spot for managing the household. The laptop computer can be closed up and stored away when not in use.

OPPOSITE: If a place to balance the checkbook and jot down and organize recipes is all you need, an area in your kitchen may be the best spot for you.

■ *The Kitchen*

The kitchen has always been the hub of the home and the favorite indoor place for discussing the day's events or trouble-shooting problems. Family members and friends alike seem to naturally gravitate to this room.

There are many options available in the kitchen for setting up a home office. The table and countertops make viable work areas, and shelves in kitchen cabinets can be reserved for storing office supplies. Unlike the dining room table, the kitchen table is designed to handle a lot of wear and tear. Still, depending on what tasks will be performed here, protecting its surface with acrylic, glass, or cardboard when you are working may be necessary. (See The Dining Room on page 48.)

NOOKS AND CRANNIES

If you don't have a full room to devote to your office, or if none of your rooms can be renovated to accommodate a home office, you will have to be more creative. Below are some locations you may not have considered before.

■ Closets

When square footage in rooms is already at a premium, allocating even a portion of that space for a home office may not be possible. The solution may lie behind closed doors. A closet may provide the space as long as it is wide enough to accommodate a workstation.

Depending on the size of the closet, you can install a freestanding desk or table or a built-in workstation. Building a workstation to fit into the area is likely to be the best use of such a small space. It allows you to use every inch of vertical and horizontal space. Shelves, drawers, and specialized compartments can store your files and equipment. Stackable plastic shelves and drawers and rolling storage carts are widely available and can be bought at discount stores or through office supply catalogs. Not only is the closet office a clever use of space, it can be hidden from view when work is done.

■ Hallways

Long considered useless space in the home (other than connecting one room to another, of course), hallways are worthy of consideration when you are looking for a spot in which to put a home office. Two areas in particular are good options: in the corner of the intersection where two hallways meet and the end of a single hallway.

Setting up in these areas won't interfere with foot traffic, as it would in a middle portion of all but the widest corridors. There's not much you can do to decorate hallways beyond hanging a few works of art or a montage of family photos.

When choosing furniture and decorations, remember that these spaces are

OPPOSITE: A walk-in closet is an ingenious location for a film-maker's studio. Built-in shelving holds various pieces of equipment, and walls are filled with momentos. Such an intimate space as this is reminiscent of a projection booth in a movie theater.

ABOVE: Tucked away in an attic alcove, this office is a secluded work space. A seat cushion makes the decorative hardwood chair more comfortable.

out in the open and should harmonize with the rest of the home's decor. In a primary-colored contemporary home, for example, a secondhand table repainted in several bold colors can complement the mood of the home while serving as a work area in the hallway. Bookcases or built-in shelving always makes sense in a hallway; they give the space the warm, homey feel of a library.

■ *Beneath the Stairs*

If your home features a main level with a staircase cantilever that creates a closet-size nook beneath, there is room for a desk, a sewing table, or other office essentials. In this case, you would probably opt to custom-build a workstation in this area in order to utilize as much space as possible in your home.

OPPOSITE: An abandoned urban commercial space that has been converted into a residential apartment offers unusual opportunities. Here, a large hallway is used for a two-person office. Stylish overhead fixtures provide direct lighting for each workstation, and ceiling fixtures brighten the space. LEFT: A small desk and shelving unit was built into this under-the-stairs location. Because the area hasn't been closed off from the entryway, both the office and the surrounding room look larger.

▨ *Butler's Pantry*

Many older homes have a butler's pantry —a small annex off the main kitchen area equipped with counter space and cabinetry. Its available square footage can be claimed for use as a home office, and its counter can become a ready-made workstation for spreading out business papers and setting up a computer or typewriter, a phone, and other necessities.

It's a wonderful place to retreat to on a Saturday morning with a cup of coffee and the paper or after dinner during the week when it's time to pay bills and get the household finances in order. For the home's primary chef, the butler's pantry is an appealing space because of its proximity to cooking areas. Pots on the stove can be watched while other jobs are being done. The pantry can be a versatile space, becoming a sewing or quilting station—or even an area in which to organize a baseball-card collection or to set up a fly-tying center. Any kind of office can be created in the butler's pantry with ease.

One of the problems you may find working in this space is insufficient lighting, as not all of these spaces will have a window or an existing light source. But because the space is probably already wired, this problem can be easily addressed by installing an overhead fixture or bringing in a strategically placed floor or table lamp.

OPPOSITE: The end of this hallway offers just enough space for a small desk and a couple of chairs. A high ceiling, plenty of natural light, and a soft, pastel yellow and blue palette make this an appealing place to work or study.

BELOW: You can tuck away a desk in the butler's pantry—if your kitchen has such a space. Shelves that once stored serving plates can hold your computer manuals and other related materials. Be careful, however, not to overload the shelves with books, which tend to be heavier than plates or dry goods.

CHAPTER THREE

SETTING THE STAGE

Like any other room in the home, your office should reflect your personal style through the principles of good interior design. Carefully consider texture, pattern, and color when decorating floors, walls, and windows. Accessorizing the space with some of your favorite things—antiques, art, collectibles, hobby gear, or personal memorabilia—will make your home office your own. This chapter will show you how to set the stage for your dream office.

WALLS

■ *Paint*

BELOW: Paint and a little imagination turned these office walls into a colorful mural. These free-form walls are, in fact, a partitioned area within a larger loft space with custom-built shelves and a desk.

OPPOSITE: A ragging technique creates a luxurious, timeworn effect in this space. A succession of glazes in varying shades of green was applied to each surface and then partially wiped with a rag. An upholstered chair adds to the charm.

These large and often very visible surfaces have great potential for creating an impact on the look of a room. They are a canvas for implementing the room's color scheme and, if desired, for conveying rhythm through pattern. Or they can be left neutral as a clean backdrop, allowing the palette and pattern to be articulated through the furnishings and accessories. Paint, wallpaper, fabric, wainscoting, and paneling are the primary choices for finishing the walls with a decorative treatment.

Paint offers many possibilities. Its colors influence the room's mood: sunny yellow creates a cheery mood; subtle gray, a serene, reflective mood. To make the most of the dominant wall color, consider accenting it with a different hue—white, to sharpen the room, or an adjacent color on the color wheel (see page 67) to create a subtle level of visual interest. A complementary color scheme is the most dramatic, but you may rule it out if you want to create another kind of atmosphere in your work environment. *(continued on page 66)*

DECORATIVE PAINT TREATMENTS

Decorative paint treatments are the new mainstays of home decorating. Stenciling, sponging, combing, and ragging are among the most popular. With some practice, you can master these do-it-yourself techniques. Any paint store can provide how-to information to help you get started—or refer you to a professional who can do the job for you. You may want a trompe l'oeil painting to create a window where there is none or to make your ceiling look like a cloud-dotted sky.

This technique is more complicated than other decorative paint treatments and requires artistic talent and patience.

Another decorative paint treatment that has been popular among homeowners is faux finishes. These centuries-old paint techniques emulate other, more elegant and expensive materials, such as various stones (granite, malachite, and marble), wood, and even leather.

OPPOSITE: The beige and violet distressed painted walls are reminiscent of an ancient ruin. The classical busts continue the theme.

ABOVE: Sponge painting in orangey tones makes this basement seem warm.

RIGHT: A trompe l'oeil sky gives this space a whimsical feel. Gold leaves on the wood beams provide a decorative contrast.

Red paint adds a bright accent to this family room office. Shelves filled with reference materials take the place of wallpaper.

Don't shy away from forest green because your office is small. Although white or a light color can make a room appear larger than it is, you are not confined to using white and light colors for small areas. When trimmed properly with a light accent, walls painted a dark, bold color can actually draw attention away from a room's size.

White or off-white creates a crisp look in a home office if the color of the accessories and furnishings is also neutral. But an all-white office can end up looking institutional and cold, so try to warm up the space with a library of books, art, or personal momentos. The grain of a warm wood floor is another good counterpoint to a sleek white room.

Once you have decided on a color, think about where you want it to be used. Paint need not be applied from floor to ceiling. You may find it more

UNDERSTANDING THE COLOR WHEEL

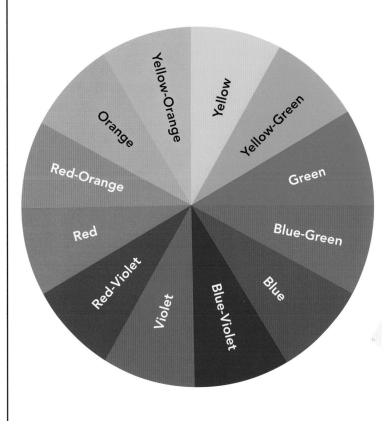

The color wheel shows how colors are related and how the source of all color is three primary colors (red, yellow, and blue), each having equal weight. By mixing each of these three primary colors with one of the others, in equal proportions, the secondary colors (orange, green, and violet) are created. Complementary colors are across the wheel from each other and make the most dramatic combinations. Adjacent colors create combinations that are the most pleasing to the eye.

interesting, especially if you are hesitant to use a strong color, to paint a dominant color only from the floor to chair-rail height. At that point, a chair-rail molding can be attached to the wall and a lighter color painted above, brightening the room and reducing the impact of the dominant color. (For a paint treatment that created a faux wainscot, see the Escaping the Bland Box Bedroom case history on page 43.)

Also think about what color the ceiling should be. For a cocoonlike effect, envelop the entire office in a single paint color. To make the ceiling virtually disappear, paint it white.

Painting the dormer window a warm red adds a lively complement to the mellow wood built-in cabinets, desk, return, and wall paneling in this office.

HELPFUL HINT
For the best results, limit the number of patterns used in your office to five. Also, be sure there's diversity in the size of the patterns: different prints that are all the same size are confusing. Try a large floral design on an area rug, a medium-size motif on a wall stencil, and a minipattern on the curtains and furniture upholstery.

■ *Wall Coverings*

When the home office should be more homelike than officelike, wall coverings can be an effective tool. More than any other wall treatment, wallpaper or fabric are soft and feminine. Also available are patterns that have sportsmens' themes such as hunting and fishing. Choosing one of these will personalize the office in a way that paint cannot.

For a conservative theme, reproductions of historic patterns give the space a timeless look. For a contemporary office, a geometric motif, a pinstripe, or a wallpaper or fabric that simulates the look of sponged paint adds a pleasing dimension to the walls. Wallpapers and fabrics can also be found in solids that have the clean look of paint but a softer textured finish.

Wall coverings can introduce pattern into a room. Because the walls dominate a room, it is essential that the pattern on the walls be fairly quiet. The goal is to select a print that enlivens the room with visual rhythm without being "busy."

RIGHT: By using the same pattern for walls, curtains, and upholstery, this room comes alive without appearing too busy. The softness of wood tones down the floral pattern.

OPPOSITE TOP: Papering the ceiling and walls in the same pattern makes an attic office feel cozy. The bright purple paper with its gold designs livens up the space.

OPPOSITE BOTTOM: The wood paneling and nautical painting are reminiscent of a ship's cabin. A fold-down desk with plenty of cubbyholes makes this an inviting place to work.

If you are not sure whether you should use wallpaper or fabric, consider some of the differences between the two materials. Wallpaper is glued to walls; fabric is stapled. Glue makes wallpaper adhere to walls securely, but it may make the paper difficult to remove as a result. Fabrics are easier to remove and offer more diversity of textures than wallpaper does. If, for example, you want the nubby texture of raw silk, fabric is a better choice than a faux silk wallpaper.

Wood Paneling and Wainscoting

If you'd like your home office to be a warm, quiet retreat with the feel of an old library or den, paneling is worth considering. The color you choose will determine the overall effect. Dark wood paneling or wainscoting adds instant authority and dignity to a home office. A lighter colored cedar or pine will lend a rustic feel to a room.

Paneled walls impart a refined elegance to this office. Unobtrusive fabric blinds let just the right amount of natural light into the room.

WINDOW TREATMENTS

Window dressings are one of the most important decorating decisions in the creation of the home office. Curtains, shades, blinds, shutters, or any combination of these must serve two functions: to admit or block sunlight and to provide privacy. They must work well and at the same time help set the style of the room.

Some windows are architecturally more attractive than others. When the window itself is not an asset to the space—when it's small, skinny, devoid of attractive trim, or awkwardly positioned—the window dressing can be designed to camouflage the imperfections and make the window more appealing. Sometimes, however, windows are the grandest architectural statement of the room. In this case, a minimalist approach should be taken when adorning the window so as not to hide its architectural beauty.

You should match the window treatment to the room's style: contemporary, traditional, country, or eclectic. For example, damask draperies ornamented with velvet braid, silk fringe, and decorative rosettes, suitable for a traditional decor, should not be considered in a streamlined contemporary setting. Vertical blinds are hard to blend into an elaborately decorated traditional setting. In a country-style room, tab curtains, simple panels made from retro fabrics, nostalgic lace panels, or even

recycled kitchen towels will fit well. In an eclectic space, almost anything goes.

One-of-a-kind window dressings can be effective in the home office that is designed as a private retreat. A trompe l'oeil mural or custom-cut wood valances, for example, can add character to a room in a way no furnishing can. If privacy is not a consideration, painting maintenance-free "curtains" around a window is a nice alternative to hanging actual curtains.

Color, pattern, and texture play an important role in window dressings. If the room's walls are already a bright, bold color, a more subtle palette may be preferred. To avoid too much of one color in the space, consult the color wheel (see page 67) to find the right complementary shades for your window dressings.

In a room without much pattern, window treatments provide an ideal opportunity to introduce pattern and, therefore, visual movement and rhythm. Remember, too, that window treatments can include more than one pattern, with prints in complementary colors used as the main fabric, lining, and trim. But if there are prints elsewhere in the decor, use patterns sparingly on windows.

Unusual muslin blinds are used as window treatments in this bedroom office. Gentle curves offset the straight lines of the walls, furniture, and black-and-white checked fabric.

Window treatments should have the appropriate texture to balance a room. For a hard, predominantly wood-filled space with few upholstered pieces, select soft, voluptuous curtain fabrics. In a carpeted room with plain drywall or plaster, wooden blinds or shades will give warmth to the space. Or you can combine a mixture of textures in a single window treatment to provide richness and depth.

OPPOSITE: Swept-up draperies add elegance to this corner home office space.

ABOVE: The diamond-mullioned window of this office is decorative by itself. The curtains that frame the window soften the angular pattern of the mullions.

LEFT: A swag provides just the right adornment in this built-in kitchen office. Tall shrubs outside ensure privacy.

HELPFUL HINT
Before you begin to decorate your office, find out if you'll need to instal additional wiring. For example, if you're going to be using a computer and a printer, a fax, and a photocopier, you may dangerously overload your electrical system. You'll want to know if you have to make wiring changes that could mean undergoing structural changes before you paint or paper your walls or lay down carpeting.

RIGHT: A moon-and-stars motif on this wall-to-wall carpeting is a delightful touch to the room with its exposed-beam ceiling and wood furnishings.

OPPOSITE: The carpet adds some pattern to this large, sleek office. It unifies the room with an expanse of soft color.

FLOORS

The floor covering for your home office can be just as varied as the walls and windows. Each floor treatment will create a different effect. It can be expensive to buy and install, so give a lot of thought to what you put under your feet.

■ *Wall-to-Wall Carpeting*

One of the most desirable flooring options, wall-to-wall carpeting brings warmth to a space. Depending on the type and the quality of the carpeting, installing wall-to-wall carpeting can be a major investment or it can be relatively inexpensive.

The cost of carpeting depends on its weight, or how many tufts of yarn per square inch (psi) the carpet has. The more tufts per square inch, the thicker and plusher the carpet, and thus the more expensive per square yard it will be. Whether a carpet is made from natural or synthetic fibers will affect the cost. Synthetic materials are now available. One made from recycled plastic bottles is surprisingly soft, but it's more expensive than carpet made from natural *(continued on page 79)*

LIGHTING

One of the most important considerations when furnishing your home office is how to light it properly. Insufficient or overwhelming lighting can result in eyestrain and fatigue.

CONTROLLING NATURAL LIGHT. Window treatments can be used to control light that spills into the room when the sun is shining brightly. Vertical or horizontal blinds, bamboo or other translucent shades, wooden shutters, or any sheer or lace draperies cut the intensity of the sun without obscuring the light.

USING ARTIFICIAL LIGHT. Even a room saturated with natural light will need other light sources—ambient and task—to be functional around the clock. Ambient light is diffused illumination that comes from a central source, usually an overhead fixture, but spreads equally throughout the space. Task lighting focuses on a particular area in which a task is to be performed. A desk lamp or reading lamp, and in some cases, track lights can be used to illuminate the work area. Position task lighting over your left shoulder if you are right-handed and over your right shoulder if you are left-handed.

To adequately light an area where you need to see well, such as for fine detail work, use a total of 2,500 lumens. For less stringent lighting needs, a total of 1,500 to 2,000 lumens is required. By adding up the lumens emitted by all the lightbulbs illuminating an area, you can make sure you are getting the amount of light

you need. Note that lumen output decreases as a lightbulb ages and can be different according to the manufacturer.

HANDLING GLARE. In a computer work area, beware of any light, natural or artificial, that produces glare. It makes it hard to see what is showing on a computer screen. Too much contrast between the dark computer screen and the light creates eyestrain by causing the eye to frequently adjust to different conditions. A light-switch dimmer and blinds or shades allow you to control the amount of light.

SPECIAL EFFECTS. Once the critical lighting has been established, you can add mood to your office with additional light sources that produce special effects. A freestanding floor lamp, or torchère, in a corner of the room adds to ambient light by producing a nice warm glow. Canister uplights that rest on the floor or a low table create a soft shower of light on a wall or a work of art, adding drama to the office. Sconces have a similar effect, producing a subtle sheen at desired intervals on the wall. Like art itself, creative lighting adds an aesthetic dimension that goes beyond the purely functional.

ABOVE: An oversize window washes this office in natural light. A decorative table lamp provides task lighting.

OPPOSITE: A large, windowed door lets in natural light which is reflected in the window facing the desk—almost doubling the amount of light. A delicate chandelier illuminates the space for nighttime work.

RIGHT: Ambient lighting is provided by decorative wall-mounted sconces while task lighting is achieved through adjustable overhead fixtures.

or other synthetic fibers. As you shop for carpeting, you will find that a cut-pile carpet is softer on the feet than a loop-pile carpet. A loop-pile carpet, however, wears better.

On the downside, carpeting traps dirt easily and needs to be cleaned often, especially if allergies are a concern. You should also bear in mind that a variegated carpet hides dirt better than a solid-color one. And before you spend a lot of money, be aware that furniture on casters moves less smoothly on plush wall-to-wall carpeting. You may be better off foregoing luxury and selecting a less expensive carpet or buying an area rug instead.

Hardwood Flooring

Considered by some to be a greater luxury than wall-to-wall carpeting, a hardwood floor is one of the most elegant choices for flooring. It is beautiful, but not necessarily practical. To protect your hardwood floor from being marred, put rubber feet on the bottom of your furniture. These inexpensive items can be purchased at any hardware store. You may also want to purchase a rubber mat to go under your chair area if your chair rides on casters.

OPPOSITE and BELOW: Hardwood floors lend rustic elegance to a space. Adding an area rug will soften the space and protect the floor from being scratched by furniture.

■ *Vinyl Tile*

Vinyl tile is one of the most practical flooring materials you can use in a home office. It comes in a variety of colors and textures—some varieties even simulate the look of hardwood flooring. Vinyl tile is durable and can be very beautiful. It is also relatively inexpensive and very easy to maintain. To protect vinyl tile, take some of the same precautions you would with hardwood floors, such as installing rubber feet and mats under furniture that moves around the office on casters.

■ *Painted Floors*

One of the hottest interior design trends today is the painted floor. If you have a special effect in mind, you can hire a professional to do the job. Painting a floor with a special technique or effect requires time, even for a professional, so be realistic before you get started.

Options in floor painting can range from checkerboards to basket-weave patterns. Or, for a whimsical effect, you can even design your own "rug."

Painting over wood planks in a checkerboard pattern gives the floor a feeling of texture. The gray-and-white color scheme is accented with a bright yellow area rug.

CASE HISTORY

MAKING THE MOST OF A SMALL SPACE

If you have a small dedicated space, the necessary equipment, and a fertile imagination, you can create a satisfying and attractive work retreat. Interior designer and editor Heather Paper had all of those ingredients when she designed her own home office.

Collaborating with Baltimore-based designer Stephen O'Brien, Paper wanted to transform a small upstairs bedroom into a highly functional and aesthetically pleasing home office. Although the room measures only 10 feet by 10 feet (3m by 3m), rich color, pattern, and a smart use of space combine to create a dream office.

"We wanted to be adventuresome," said O'Brien. This meant starting with a dramatic but neutral core of essentials—black modular office furniture. Because black is a "noncolor," it freed up the palette for a wide range of hues.

The walls are wrapped in a delicious melon hue inspired by a bold Southwestern-style fabric print that makes a contemporary statement in the office. A guest chair opposite the desk—a sociable feature every dream office should include—is dressed in the same geometric print.

In lieu of traditional drapery treatments, fabric-covered screens add one-of-a-kind flavor and make the room's ceiling height seem higher than 8 feet (2.5m). (The use of folding screens is a design trick that creates a feeling of spaciousness when in fact space is limited.)

"When you have an office at home, there needs to be a break in the design flow to represent getting away to the office. You need to separate work and home," O'Brien says, explaining the office's mood swing from the rest of the house.

With attractive, efficient storage units as well as a computer that can be connected to the Internet, this home office satisfies all the criteria for becoming more than a merely functional space; thanks to its design and practicality, it enters the realm of dream office—all 100 square feet (9.5 sq m) of it.

Vertical lines and warm Southwestern colors make this pint-size office seem larger than it is.

■ *Area Rugs*

Area rugs will add warmth to the floor and protect it from heavy foot traffic. They should be placed in a spot where sliding chairs won't have to make a transition from floor to rug.

FINISHING THE SPACE

After you've finished decorating your office, it's time to go shopping for the furnishings and equipment that you need. Then, to complete the job, decorate your new home office with artwork, antiques, vases, statues, figurines, books, clocks, houseplants, fresh flowers, or whatever else comes to mind. Chapters 4 and 5 will help you get the job done well.

LEFT: A custom-made rug with spirals and jagged geometric shapes is the perfect finishing touch in this office. The colors of the various shapes in the rug brighten the space.

BELOW: A rug with a Far Eastern flavor adds warmth to this room and protects the hardwood floor from being scratched by the chair and the wooden table that serves as a desk.

WORKING WITH TEXTURES

Some rooms have it, some don't: that extra touch of style that makes a space sing with life. By paying attention to the look and feel of the various components, you can transform your home office space from an ordinary one into an extraordinary one.

CREATE INTEREST THROUGH CONTRAST. A home is compelling when it is decorated with eclectic style. Place a twig basket on top of a file cabinet or a glass tabletop to create textural contrast and the visual interest that goes with it. Or counter the rustic warmth of a collection of rough-hewn wood folk-art birdhouses by displaying them near a window dressed with soft, flowing, sheer or lightweight cotton curtains.

DON'T FORGET THE WARMTH OF WOOD. Wood is inherently cozy. The home office may feel a bit on the "cold" side because of its office equipment and upholstered desk chair. Try to include a wood chair, a wooden lamp, or a handcrafted wooden accessory in your office.

USE ROUGH TEXTURES FOR A RUSTIC, CASUAL STYLE. Rough-textured materials, such as twigs, cedar, natural canvas, and punched tin, work a magic all their own. They give a room an untamed yet inviting feel. Used sparingly as accents, these materials add just a hint of wildness.

SOFTEN SPACES WITH FABRIC. If a tabletop displays a grouping of favorite wooden decoys, for example, consider softening the impact by covering the table with fabric. The contrast between the wood and the soft, undulating folds of fabric will call attention to the decoys. And instead of placing wooden furnishings directly on a wood floor, soften the setting with a woven area rug.

ABOVE: Wood furniture and a kitchen island soften the look of the cool masonry floor in this apartment. OPPOSITE: Dark cherry wood is a mellow contrast to the light oak floor.

CHAPTER FOUR

FURNISHING THE SPACE

The furniture you choose for your office space should be functional, but keep in mind that it will also influence the feel of the space. Upholstery fabrics and furniture finishes and materials will have a great impact on how your space will look. This chapter will help you purchase and arrange your office furniture.

ARRANGING OFFICE FURNITURE

Now that you have found a home for your office and have established a decorating scheme, you are ready to consider the arrangement of furniture and equipment—the office layout. The following sample layout ideas will help you to plan your workstation. Once that area is defined, you can arrange additional seating, tables, and other furnishings with ease.

■ *The Wall Layout*

A wall layout sets all work-related furniture and equipment flush against one wall. Areas in which this type of layout is ideal include multipurpose rooms, as well as rooms with just enough space left over for a table and chairs or perhaps a sofa. This layout is especially appealing when you're considering building the office furnishings into the wall. The simple linear design is easy to construct, and if a window happens to be in the middle of the wall, the furniture on either side can create a nice symmetrical balance. In addition, the wall layout is a clean, streamlined layout for a home office.

Consider, however, that you will not have all work-related materials within easy reach. Being able to reach behind or to either side of the work area to access files is often an important convenience. *(continued on page 92)*

BELOW and OPPOSITE: The wall layout is a simple arrangement that works especially well in a room with a long, uninterrupted wall and is ideal when the office requires more than one workstation. The setup below is sleek and streamlined while the office on the opposite page has a softer look, with a built-in workstation that is curved to fit the curved walls.

SKETCHING YOUR OFFICE LAYOUT

Draw a map of the room that you have chosen to use as an office. This will prove invaluable to you when determining how you want the space to look. Make sure you have the following materials at hand:

■ GRAPH PAPER

■ A RULER OR T-SQUARE

■ A COMPASS

■ A TRIANGLE

■ PENCILS AND ERASERS

Graph paper with ¼- to ½-inch (6 to12mm) squares. Each square will represent one square foot (.09 sq m) of actual floor space, so choose the larger ½-inch-square paper if you want a larger-scale rendering to work from; however, most professional floor plans are executed on graph paper with ¼-inch (6mm) squares. For the neatest job, attach your graph paper to a clipboard with masking tape to keep it from moving. A ruler or T-square for drawing straight horizontal lines, a compass for drawing the arcs of open doors, a triangle for drawing true vertical lines, pencils and erasers.

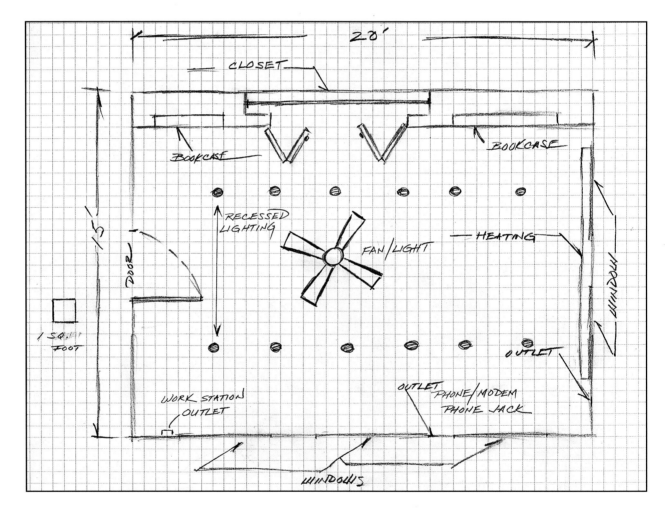

USING A ROUGH SKETCH

A rough sketch helps you understand how you can organize your space. The room measurements you've noted will give you an idea of what size furniture and equipment will fit in the space.

On a piece of paper, sketch the perimeters of the room, but not to scale. Then measure each wall and transfer the measurements onto your rough sketch. Indicate all windows and doors, electrical outlets, phone jacks, heating vents, closets, and changes in elevation. To record the windows, measure from one corner of the wall to the outer edge of the window, and from the other outer edge to the other corner of the wall.

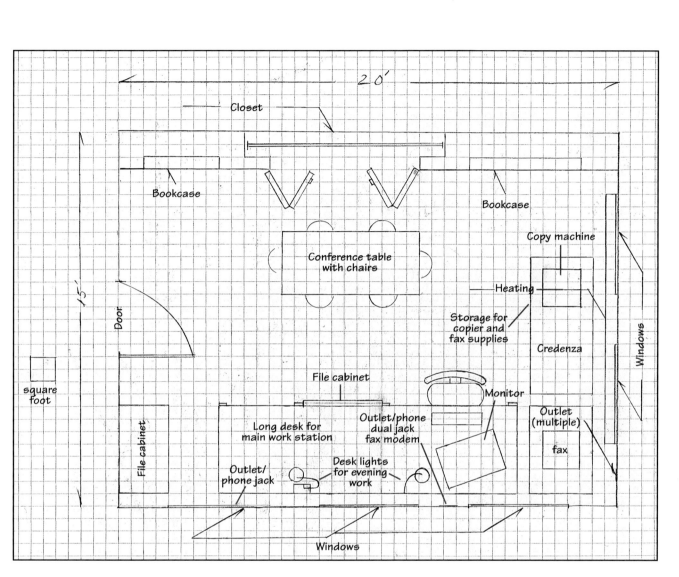

FINAL FLOOR PLAN

Once you have answered your questions and solved the problems that you discovered during the rough sketch stage, you are ready for a final floor plan. A floor plan is helpful even if you don't build in a unit. The measurements you make for the floor plan will ensure that the furnishings you buy will fit and how much open space will remain. The open space is just as important as the space occupied by furnishings and equipment. You'll want to make sure you have enough room to move around in your chair, for example.

For each ¼- or ½-inch (6 or 12mm) square on the paper, designate a single square foot (.09 sq m) of floor space. For a wall that measures 10 feet 3 inches (3.1m), draw a line with your ruler or T-square that includes 10 squares. Use the triangle to draw accurate, perfectly straight lines. To designate the area occupied by a door, measure the door's width, then draw an arc to show in which direction the door swings open.

ABOVE: The parallel layout works well in this casual office. Files and supplies are neatly stored in straw baskets within easy reach directly behind the work area.

RIGHT: Like the wall layout, but with an extension, the L-shaped layout is an efficient setup that serves to free up space in the middle of a room. Here the work area takes full advantage of the wall of windows.

Parallel Layout

The parallel layout adds to the wall layout by arranging a desk parallel to file cabinets or the computer setup. The desk is placed away from the wall and faced toward the center of the room; the wall behind the desk is devoted to storage and equipment.

The parallel layout is ideal for the person who wants to keep the desk free of office equipment. If the office is to be used as a meeting place for conferences with clients, this layout has the advantage of allowing discussions over a desk unencumbered with the mechanics of work. Chairs for clients can be easily placed in front of the desk.

L-Shaped Layout

When little space is available for key office elements, an L-shaped layout may be helpful. Corners are often underutilized; by wrapping around a corner, this layout puts otherwise dead space to

A desk chair on casters and a smooth floor of vinyl tile or hard wood with a protective cover will help you move from one end of the workstation to the other.

good use. This plan also provides room for the necessary office functions in an efficient style.

Although the L-shaped layout is most often implemented in a corner against two walls, it doesn't have to be. In a large room, the L-shaped office area can be positioned in the center.

■ *Horseshoe Layout*

The horseshoe, or U-shaped, layout is as popular as it is efficient. Not only does this set-up offer optimum counter space with three surfaces for spreading out work materials, but by featuring two sides that wrap around (or behind) a desk/work area, all office functions can be easily tended to without your having to get up.

Within the horseshoe layout, several options are possible. The desk can be located in the center of the U arrangement, with additional tables/countertops extending at each side to the rear. Or an L-shaped table area can be built into the corner of the room, following the perimeters of two walls, with a free-standing desk forming the third side of the horseshoe.

In a larger office, the horseshoe layout frees up the remaining space for other furnishings. And when the office

OFFICE FURNITURE CHECKLIST

■ desk/workstation

■ credenza

■ filing cabinet

■ shelving unit

■ chairs

■ sofa

■ conference table

The horseshoe layout puts all the office equipment within reach. Here, a curved desk softens the hard edges of the work surface.

shares space in a large room designed for another purpose, the horseshoe layout easily delineates the office from the remainder of the room.

FURNITURE STYLES

Furniture styles are as varied as any other element of design. To set a mood, or to best suit the function of your office, you can choose from the following options.

■ *Custom Built-in Furniture*

Most of the four types of office layouts on pages 90–96 can include built-in furniture. If the wall you are building on, however, is obstructed by an off-center window or other architectural element, furniture on either side of the window may throw the room off balance visually. Be sure to draft your ideas for built-ins to scale on graph paper first to decide whether the results are satisfactory and worth pursuing

This built-in wall unit is customized to fit a large library of hardcover reference books and periodicals. Niches were included for small art objects, making the unit both beautiful and functional.

(see Sketching Your Office Layout on pages 92–93 and Designing Built-in Furniture on pages 106–107.)

To maximize square footage, try an L-shaped layout with built-in furniture. If built into a corner, a large desk/countertop can be placed along one wall, with a shorter ell on the adjoining wall.

The materials you use should be durable, attractive, and affordable. Inexpensive wood or wood-product building materials won't be as durable or able to bear heavy loads as more expensive materials will. If stored items are lightweight, the cheaper materials will suffice. When painted, they can complement the overall room scheme.

■ *Ready-made Office Furniture*

The popularity of the personal computer has spawned a wide range of furnishings designed to support budding home offices around the world.

This compact stand-alone unit includes a sleek desk, some shelves, drawers for supplies, and even filing cabinets.

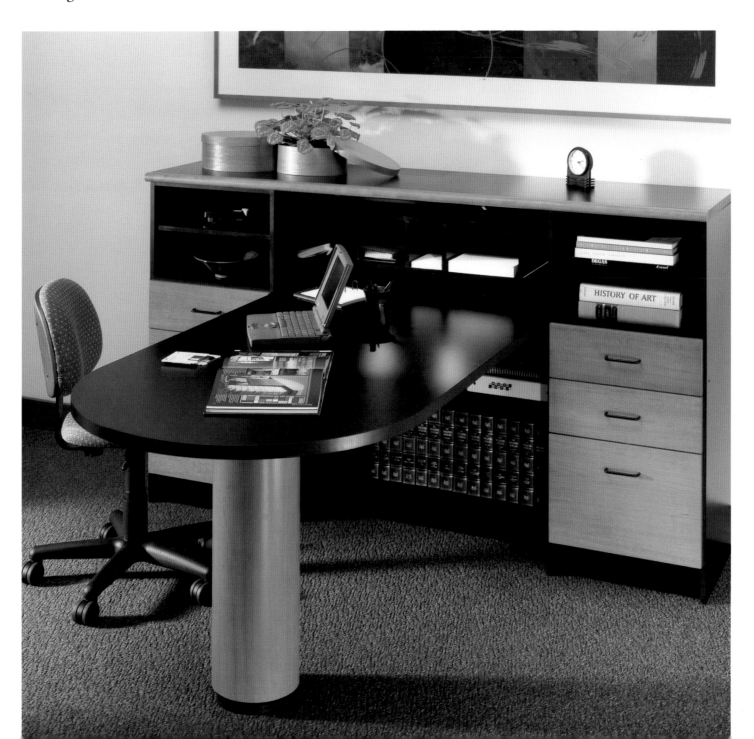

RIGHT: In an open office space located in the living room of this home, a high-backed chair on casters and a supply cart do not detract from the clean white-and-wood decor. A black-and-white area rug was selected to connect the ready-made furnishings to the rest of the room.

OPPOSITE: An antique-style desk with little compartments makes a charming statement as well as provides many separate niches for storing various supplies, from pencils to paper clips.

A variety of computer furniture is available—from roll-around tables with slide-out drawers for keyboards and bridges for monitors to L-shaped corner units that allow the printer to be placed to the side of the main desktop. Space-saving options include stacked systems in which drawers that hold the keyboard and the printer slide out when they are in use and slide back for behind-doors storage when the workday is done.

Furnishing the home with ready-made pieces can make your space look more like a workplace than a home. When a room is devoted to the home office, this consideration may not be important. However, when the office is sharing space in a room, office furnishings should be compatible with the other pieces in the room. Fortunately, major advances have been made in designing home office furniture that's aesthetically pleasing as well as functional. This is especially true if the room's decor is contemporary. A wide selection of office furnishings will blend pleasingly with the decor—and even enhance it.

■ *Traditional Furniture*

Nothing warms a room more than the ambience of the past. An antique library table or a classic oak rolltop desk can enrich the work experience. Other easy-to-find pieces you may want to consider include bookcases made of oak with glass doors; oak file cabinets (be sure these are wide enough to accommodate *(continued on page 101)*

NATURAL VERSUS MANMADE FABRICS—PROS AND CONS

The fabrics you choose for your home office furniture and curtains should be functional and pleasing.
A luxurious fabric may not wear well in an office setting. It may feel scratchy, fade, or stain easily. Synthetic fabrics
tend to be heat-sensitive. A fabric that is light sensitive will fade. Below is a list of different fabrics you can consider,
along with their advantages and drawbacks.

Fabric	Pros	Cons
NATURAL FIBERS		
Cotton	durable, adaptable, takes dye easily, colorfast, can be cleaned easily	shrinks, wrinkles, stains easily
Leather/Suede	durable, creates a dignified atmosphere	expensive, easily ruined, not easily cleaned
Linen	strong, durable, neutral	shrinks, wrinkles, expensive
Silk	elegant, soft, beautiful	expensive, light-sensitive, not color-fast, fragile
Wool	warm look and feel, naturally absorbent, retains body heat	subject to attack by moths, scratchy feel
SYNTHETIC FIBERS		
Acetate	adaptable	heat-sensitive, stains easily, low durability
Acrylic	soft, warm, durable, mothproof, stain-resistant	heat-sensitive
Nylon	strong, wrinkle-resistant, stretches easily	stains easily, heat-sensitive
Polyester	low absorbency, durable	does not stretch, feels coarse

RIGHT: A striped cotton fabric is draped in an arch around this window. Colorfast cotton is a good choice for this sunny space. The plush bedspread, blanket, and pillows adds to the luxuriousness of the space.

OPPOSITE: Corduroy, a raised-pile fabric made of cotton, makes a soft durable covering for a chair.

your files) with their original hardware; and simple benches (for spreading out papers and files or organizing stacks of books or magazines). It is often more costly to furnish your office this way, but the look and feel that these pieces give your office are worth the trouble.

■ *Multipurpose Furnishings*

When your home office is set up in the dining room or living room, multipurpose home furniture that doesn't glaringly say "office" may be preferred. For example, an old-fashioned rectangular farm table or primitive pine worktable with drawers can do double duty for both dining and office needs. Pencils, papers, rulers, stapler, paper clips, and other small office supplies can be stashed out of sight in the drawers when the table serves the dining function. Similarly, a pie safe or closed-door cupboard situated near the table/desk complements the dining room decor and provides storage for smaller pieces.

In the living or family room or in the bedroom, the home office component can blend inconspicuously into the room's design scheme in the form of a home entertainment center. This multipurpose furnishing can house a television set and stereo while also providing a desk space and storage for computer components.

When choosing multipurpose furnishings, remember that there's no single solution. The key is to select furniture that will blend with your decorating scheme while still meeting the necessary office function.

■ *Outfitting Other Areas of the Office*

After you've determined which kind of furnishings are best for your work space, it's time to decide how to furnish the rest of the room. Choices will differ depending on how you intend to use the space.

If you plan to have meetings with clients or family, you will want to include an extra chair or two, pulled close to the desk to facilitate eye contact and a sense of intimacy. The type of chair you choose should reflect the atmosphere you want to create for those who will be seated in it. A soft, "sink-down" *(continued on page 104)*

(continued on page 104)

OPPOSITE: Traditional-style office furniture and accessories blend the workspace into the decor of the home.

ABOVE: In the corner of an apartment, an armoire houses a computer station and pull-out shelf for the keyboard. Paperwork and receipts are filed away in binders and boxes.

THE DESK CHAIR

The one piece of office furniture you should choose with extra care is the desk chair. It must be comfortable, or you will likely develop backaches, leg cramps, and fatigue. A handsome straight-back chair or easy chair is not usually a good choice. The best office desk chair is designed to be ergonomically correct, with contours that conform to (and can be adjusted to fit) your back, legs, and seat. This ensures that you can sit for many hours in comfort. As a rule, the more ergonomically correct a chair's design and construction is, the more expensive it is. You can cut corners elsewhere to stay within your budget, but don't compromise here.

Visit several office furniture stores and try out a variety of chairs before you buy. An ergonomic design should offer a firm but comfortable seat and back. The seat should be somewhat rounded at the front and the back contoured only for support. The seat height should also be adjustable. The chair should respond to your movements, moving forward or backward with you as your body shifts and moves while you're seated. Upholstery fabric should be soft, not scratchy, and it should breathe. It should provide proper lumbar support and have a footrest if desired.

If you work at a computer all day long, you may find that an armless chair is more comfortable, especially if you have a pad to rest your forearms on. However, armrests provide valuable support for your elbows which, when you work at a computer, are in a bent position for long periods of time. A swivel seat and casters will enable you to have access to everything you need in your office without getting up, but if all needed materials are located within arm's reach, a stationary chair will probably suffice.

In some cases, the more expensive a desk chair is, the more comfortable it will be (right), but less expensive models with arm rests and good lumbar support also make great choices (above).

easy chair produces a relaxed environment, whereas a more formal, less cushioned chair conveys a seriousness of purpose. Also consider the height of the chairs that will be facing your desk. Do you want to convey that you are clearly in charge? If so, select chairs for guests of a lower seat height than your desk chair. Otherwise, choose chairs whose height is similar to yours.

A small arrangement of table and chairs is a great idea if you plan to have frequent conferences in your office. A square or round table offers a democratic setting, provides space on which to spread out papers, and facilitates note taking at meetings.

Add a sofa or love seat to your design for those times when you'll want an intimate atmosphere for more informal meetings without the barrier of a desk. You may want to include this larger seating option for your own comfort even if you don't need it for visitors. Stretching out on the sofa is a nice break from organizing tax information for the accountant. If space permits, put a coffee table or an occasional table in front of your sofa for papers, beverages, or snacks.

RIGHT: This armoire opens out to become a workstation. When closed, the colors and texture of the wood enhance the room's natural decor.

OPPOSITE: If you will be meeting with clients in your office, create a comfortable environment. In this space, a meeting can take place around the octagonal table when papers need to be spread out. For an informal business conference, the sofa can be used.

DESIGNING BUILT-IN FURNITURE

Before installing built-in furniture in your office, it is important to determine how you can best use the space. For example, floor-to-ceiling bookshelves can include a desk area. Estimate shelf heights and determine how much of the wall unit should be devoted to open and closed shelving (shelves, drawers, and cabinets). Also figure in the dimensions of office equipment, including lamps, computers, and a fax, and for wiring (preferably concealed from sight). See Sketching Your Office Layout on pages 92–93 for guidance.

If need be, a built-in unit can serve more than just the office function. It can also display collectibles and books, and accommodate a TV set and sound system. A built-in office shelving system offers flexibility because you customize it to your specific needs. You can, for example, include narrow drawers suitable for storing computer diskettes or special compartments for storing hobby items such as spools of thread.

ABOVE and RIGHT: Wood shelves make a home office seem more like a library. Formica (right) makes the office seem streamlined and efficient.

CHAPTER FIVE

ESSENTIAL EQUIPMENT

The office equipment you buy is, of course, of major importance. In this day of ever-evolving technology, be sure to research each piece of equipment you buy—you don't want to find yourself with obsolete equipment sooner than later.

HELPFUL HINT
A personal computer requires a cool climate or it may malfunction. Make sure your office will not become overheated and that the computer is not in close proximity to a heat source.

A COMPUTER FOR YOU

If you are new to computing, purchase only basic hardware: a CPU (central processing unit) or hard drive, a monitor, a keyboard, a mouse, and a printer. Personal computers are designed to perform many functions, from checkbook balancing to desktop publishing. As you become familiar with your new system, you will find out what other equipment and software programs you may want. You may want to hire a consultant to help you decide what you'll need to buy. *(continued on page 114)*

RIGHT: This computer workstation has a keyboard and a mouse that are stored on a pullout shelf that is out only when it's in use.

OPPOSITE: The monitor, fax, and printer are all positioned on either side of the desk, leaving plenty of space in the center for paperwork.

SETTING UP A COMPUTER

If you have an L-shaped office or horseshoe layout (see pages 92–94), you should position your system according to whether you're right- or left-handed. A right-handed person should place the keyboard and monitor on the right; a left-handed person to the left.

A variety of computer "desks" are widely available. They are usually built to specifications that are different from standard desks. They enable you to place the monitor and keyboard at a comfortable distance. If yours is a large-screen monitor (17 inches [43cm] or larger), you will want to be especially careful that the monitor is low enough. Looking up at it can cause neck strain, headaches, and backaches.

The best way to position a keyboard is to place it slightly lower than standard desk height. The optimum position is 24 to 27 inches (60 to 69cm) from the floor (with some leeway for individual body types). Also be sure that there's plenty of unrestricted leg room—about 24 inches (60cm) in width.

ABOVE: This store-bought work-station puts monitor and keyboard at the right height.

OPPOSITE: In this computer setup the keyboard slides out of sight when not needed.

KEY COMMUNICATORS

Communication is often the most essential aspect of running a successful business. Here are some of the most common and crucial devices.

▦ *Telephones*

A wall-mounted phone frees up desk space and is an efficient choice if you need as much surface area as possible. But if that's not an issue, you may wish to avoid the extra reach that's required to answer and hang up a wall phone and choose a desk model instead.

Phones come in all shapes and sizes (and colors), so it's important to find one that's the right weight and shape for you. Hold the receiver in your hand and up to your ear before buying the phone. Sometimes the most appealing novelty phones are more fun to look at than they actually are to use. Be sure the buttons are the right size. Nothing is more frustrating than discovering that they're too small to be pressed accurately and quickly, or even to be read properly.

Today's phones are available with a range of features. The speakerphone feature is worth the extra money if you want to have your hands free when you are talking. Speakerphones are also useful for impromptu conference calls. Before purchasing a phone with this feature, test it to make sure the speaker function is clear and has an adequate range. A redial feature comes in handy should you get a busy signal and need

to continue trying to reach your party. Many phone models offer a "frequently called numbers" feature. This allows you to program the phone numbers you dial most often into the memory so that you need to punch only one or two keys to reach those numbers. When the button or buttons are pressed, the number is automatically dialed for you.

If you want to be free to talk on the phone while working on-line, or if you receive a high volume of calls, you will need to have the telephone company install a second phone line. You can also purchase a headset that you can wear comfortably all day. A cordless phone or a cellular phone with its own phone number (and monthly bill), which you can take along with you when you leave the house, will give you added flexibility. Consider investing in a neck-cradle attachment for your receiver to reduce neck strain. Other features you may want to add to your phone system include a built-in answering machine and/or a fax machine. These models are expensive, but the space savings make them well worth the money. They cost about the same as purchasing the three units separately and are worth the investment if every square inch counts in your home office.

▦ *Answering Machines*

A wide range of features for answering machines is available, so compare several models before making a choice. Some options include call screening, which lets you know who's calling before you

answer the phone. You may want a digital display of the number of new messages recorded. Some machines limit the length of a message; others allow the caller to talk as long as needed. Many answering machines have an access code that can be dialed when you're away from home, allowing you to receive your messages wherever you are.

Voice mail, an alternative to the answering machine, is a service now available through many local phone companies. This service eliminates the need for an extra piece of machinery cluttering up your home office, and it is available at a nominal fee. Always do research to find out which option is best for you.

■ Fax Machines

Most businesses swear by fax machines. Faxing is immediate—with the speed of a phone call, printed information can be delivered to the recipient. An insurance claim report can be sent to your insurer at once, speeding up the process of reimbursement for a loss. Memos, letters, and reports can be delivered and received, and deadlines can be met.

Technology makes today's home offices powerful. All you need is some equipment and a few square feet and you can instantly communicate with anyone in the world and even send them electronic files via the Internet.

HELPFUL HINT
A surge protector is a necessary investment to protect your computer system and can be purchased relatively inexpensively at your local computer store.

Faxes require only a standard phone jack, plus a nearby electrical outlet for plugging in both the phone and the fax's copy function. Two basic fax models include the single-sheet and the self-cutting-paper machines. Multiple documents received on a single-sheet machine will arrive to you on one continuous sheet of paper with cut marks delineating each page's end. These are a little more time-consuming than the self-cutting machines. If you want your pages individually separated, you will have to use scissors to cut them apart.

Software is also available that allows your computer modem to act as your fax. You can receive documents right onto your computer screen—you need to print them out only if necessary. This option will help you free up valuable counter space in your home office. The major drawback with this fax option is that the only documents you will be able to send are those generated on your computer.

OTHER OFFICE HELPERS

This office has specific workstations. On the left is a drafting table and phone. In the center filing cabinets and a photocopier are accessible to anyone who needs them. On the right is a dedicated computer station and a table used for meetings and paperwork.

Aside from communication devices, you will need to furnish your office with other equipment to keep your operation running smoothly. Here are just a few machines you may want to include.

This horseshoe layout has a computer, printer, fax, and filing cabinets installed along a rear wall, leaving the other two sides clear for paperwork. A sleek desk lamp sits at one corner of the desk, but provides light to the center of the writing area.

■ *Copy Machines*

You may want to consider buying a small copier for your home office. If you are running a business, the convenience of being able to make copies without leaving your home will increase efficiency dramatically, making this piece of equipment worth its expense.

Not too long ago, only large businesses had copy machines, and the equipment was always massive and

expensive. But along with technology's advances in other areas of equipment, the copier has come a long way. Today a small desktop model occupying only about 18 square inches (46cm) is available. One convenient model uses a removable cartridge that contains the toner, developer, and drum, eliminating the need for you to replace these materials individually. The cartridge, which is available from any office supply store, is replaced after a certain number of copies have been made on the machine. Other copiers have separate toner and developer compartments, making them somewhat less convenient to maintain. Both the cartridge and toner models use ordinary paper.

A dry copier requires no toner or developer. Less expensive than the other models, this one utilizes a special coated paper, which drives up the cost per copy as a trade-off for the initial lower cost. For considerably more money, copiers that print in color are available.

Copiers feature a range of options from simple to sophisticated. Before buying or leasing, find out how long the machine takes to warm up and how long it takes to make copies (if you're always in a hurry, these features will be of prime importance). Look into the maintenance and the type of paper that is required. Machines are also available with both single-sheet and automatic paper feed (if you frequently copy documents that are many pages long, the latter feature can be very helpful). Other options to look for include the machine's ability to copy on different sizes of paper and a reduction and enlargement feature.

If you will only need to occasionally make a copy of an insurance document or a check, you won't need a separate copy machine. A combination telephone, answering machine, and fax machine (see Telephones on page 114) includes a copier function. Consider purchasing a fax machine that uses plain copy paper.

■ *Calculators*

The calculator is an important piece of equipment for any home office. The most desirable models include both a digital display of the calculations and a paper printout. The paper printout is a feature you will appreciate when keeping track of the household budget and doing your taxes. Most calculators operate on either AC current or batteries. Some are solar-powered.

When making your selection, be certain the keys are large enough, with adequate spacing in between, to fit your fingers. Keys that are too small or too close together can result in mistakes. Choose a model that has a clearly readable display and a legible printout.

This bracket-and-board shelving system is adjustable. For maximum use of space, oversize items like books are stored horizontally. Beneath the shelves there is room for a fax and a wire file folder.

TIPS ON STORAGE AND FILING

If your job or hobby involves a lot of small items, such as swatches or beads, or very large items, such as maps, building plans, or artwork, storing them well takes a little creativity. For inspiration on all types of storage solutions, browse through flea markets, antique shops, stationery stores, and office-supply stores. Here are some options to consider:

STORING SMALL ITEMS. A large jewelry box or an antique box may be the right size and have the number of compartments you need. A pharmaceutical cabinet also has compartments and will hold objects of various sizes. If the items are thin, you can tuck them into glassine sleeves that photographers use for transparencies and store them in a binder on a shelf.

OVERSIZE PAPER AND FABRIC. If these can be rolled into a cylinder without being damaged, roll them up and insert them into a decorative oversize vase or umbrella stand. If whatever you are storing must lie flat, you'll need to invest in a flat file or a wall-mounted display unit, such as the ones used by stores to display posters.

PORTABLE FILES AND SHELVES. A variety of file storage units on wheels are available at most office-supply stores. Most are small, with two tiers of hanging files. If you'd like to recycle a bookcase that you already have, or if you need a larger portable unit, you can buy a set of castors at a hardware store, turn the unit upside down, and install the wheels. It is important to prevent items from falling off the shelves when you move the unit from place to place and that the shelves and the wheels be sturdy.

ABOVE: An extra piece of furniture isn't necessary when files and equipment can be tucked away in pull-out drawers.

OPPOSITE: Wicker baskets are a low-tech alternative to industrial-looking metal or plastic filing cabinets.

GETTING ORGANIZED

If you work at home, chances are good that you do more than one job in your office. You have at least two arenas of activity—household matters and business affairs. Keeping these two separate from each other—and keeping them organized—is something of an art. Some people rely on their computer and software to get the job done; others feel more comfortable using more familiar everyday tools. Here are some low-tech ideas that use common items to help get you more organized.

COLOR-CODING FILES. If you manage the household, do volunteer work for a charity, and run a part-time business, you may find that giving each segment of your life it's own color will help you find things faster. You might consider, for example, green for business, blue for your home files, and yellow or white for the charity work.

KEEPING NAMES AND NUMBERS. You can also code phone/address cards using the above color system. If you prefer to use a standard pocket address book, you can use a different color ink for each part of your life.

SPIRAL NOTEBOOKS. Avoid all those little "To Do" lists. Use a spiral notebook and mark a ruled line down the center of each page. Jot down your tasks for the household on one side and for your business on the other. Or, if you would like more space for them, allot one page for each, with the left-hand page for home and the right-hand page one for business. If one list runs longer than the other, use a large paper clip to secure the pages together for easy reference.

BUSINESS FOLDER. If you use a spiral notebook (see above) to take notes during meetings, you can insert it into a leather folder. These folders often come with side pockets for storing phone lists with frequently used numbers and a calendar. Some even house a calculator. Be sure to date the notes of each entry and add the names of those attending the meeting. This can became a running log and help you remember what needs to be done.

MAIL CALL. It is best to have two places for mail, one for home and one for business, and keep a trash can nearby for unwanted junk mail. Try to handle each piece of mail only twice—once when you sort it and again when you deal with it.

TAX RECEIPTS. Keep two files (color coded as indicated above), one for personal matters, one for business. When you acquire a receipt, jot down on the receipt what it is in reference to and tuck it into the appropriate folder. Tape small receipts that can easily get lost to an 8½ x 11 piece of paper. When tax time comes around, you'll find it's much easier to access and interpret your receipts.

CHECKLISTS AND LOGS. If you are handling several complicated projects at once, make a master log or make one for each project and include all the pertinent steps or stages and target completion dates and deadlines. It's a great feeling to check off a task after you've completed it.

MASTER SHOPPING LIST. Compose a master shopping list of all the supplies you need and make a dozen photocopies of it. Each week (or month, depending on how fast you deplete supplies) circle each item as it needs replenishing on one of the copies. When it is time to go shopping, you can take your list with needed items indicated with you. It's a good idea to specify important information on the master list, such as a brand name, size, or model type (as for a computer printer cartridge). You'll never come home with the wrong item and you may even be able to recruit someone to do the shopping for you. (This is also a good idea for grocery shopping. For the best results, organize regularly bought items by aisle in the store.)

WORKSTATIONS. Analyze each workstation in your office and buy sufficient supplies and equipment for each. For example, at your fax station place a stapler, a staple remover, a pen-on-a-string, and a phone list of frequently used fax numbers within easy reach. A lot of time and energy can be conserved if you don't have to go to the fax, return to your desk, find what you need, and then return to the fax.

TRY BARTERING. Use the barter system to enlist office help. If filing and organizing are not your strong points, consider exchanging your time and talent with a friend. If you can offer a needed service in exchange for an organized friend's time and expertise, you've gained a lot at little cost to you.

OPPOSITE: This combination unit with shelves and pull-out filing drawers offers flexibility. You can vary the shelf heights and even add another shelf if desired.

LEFT: A closet with deep pull-out bins can neatly hold a variety of items from a magazine collection to office supplies to old files. The least used items should go in the top drawer.

SOURCES

pages 2-3
Jefferson Riley
Centerbrook Architects
67 Main St.
Centerbrook, CT 06409

pages 8, 9, 50
Knight Associates
Beach Hill Rd.
Blue Hill, ME 04614

pages 10-11
David Parker
New York, NY

pages 17 bottom, 34, 35,
    73 top
Richard Wiles
Houses and Interiors
(44) 171 336-7942

page 19
Robert Davis, AIA
Design One of Edina, Ltd.
4010 W. 65th St. Suite 217
Edina, MN 55435

pages 26-27
Dick Dudley
Concord, NH

page 26 left
Lasar Architects
Box 1401
New Milford, CT 06776

pages 29 right, 30
House Beautiful
224 W. 57 St. 4th Floor
New York, NY 10019

page 31
Brassard Design Assoc.
88 E. Bergen Pl.
Red Band, NJ 07701

pages 36-37, 63-64, 68
Charles Riley
New York
(212) 647-9128
Los Angeles
(213) 931-1134

pages 42, 65 top
Philip Harvey
Osburn Design
200 Kansas Street
Suite #208
San Francisco, CA 94103
415-487-2333

pages 44, 70, 102 left
The Knoll Group
1235 Water Street
East Greenville, PA 18041
1-800-445-5045

pages 45
Winter Panel Corp.
Box 168 B RR 5
Battleboro, VT 05301

page 46
Bernardo Urquieta
(415) 989-2433

pages 49 top, 88
Kar Ho
117 West 17 St., Suite 4H
New York, NY 10011

pages 50 right, 80, 110 left,
    112, 113
IKEA
B.V. Service Inc.
Plymouth Common
496 Germantown Pike
Plymouth Meeting, PA 19462
610-834-0180

page 53
Kitchens by Deane
1267 E. Main St.
Stanford, CT 06902

page 55
Chad Floyd
Centerbrook Architects
67 Main St.
Centerbrook, CT 06409

pages 58, 77 top
American Home Style
Magazine
375 Lexington Ave
New York, NY 10017

pages 60-61
Paul H. Kim
403 East 77 St., Suite 5
New York, NY 10021

page 69 top
Frank A. Lavin, Jr.
25 Logan St.
Denver, CO 80203

page 71
Frank Israel
254 S. Robertson Blvd.
Los Angeles, CA 90211

page 72
Patricia Bonis
8 Fairway Ct.
Cresskill, NJ 07626

page 74
Deborah Lipner, Ltd.
1 Fawcett Pl.
Greenwich, CT 06902

page 76
Brian Murphy
147½ West Channel
Santa Monica, CA 90402

page 77 bottom
Celeste Cooper
New York, NY
(212) 826-5667

pages 79, 92 bottom, 105
Jane Davis Doggett
303 S. Beach Rd.
Jupiter Island, Hope Sound,
    FL 33455

page 95
Techline
Marshall Erdman & Associates
5117 University Avenue
P.O. Box 5249
Madison, WI 53705
608-238-0211

page 106 left
VanBeuren/Webb Architects
1133 Broadway, Suite 611
New York, NY 10010

pages 116-117
Carla Schrad
9725 Green Oak Dr.
Los Angeles, CA 90068

Index

PHOTO CREDITS

©William Abranowicz/A+C Anthology: pp. 96, 101

©Christopher C. Bain: p. 67 top

BDH Advertising: ©Neville Johnson: p. 67

©Bjorg: pp. 49 top, 88 (Stylist: Andrew Lee; Architect: Kar Ho), 60-61 (Collection of Paul Kim), 106 left (Design by Van Beuren/Webb Architects)

©Hedrich Blessing, photo by Nick Merrick: 33

©Kelly Bugden: pp. 121

©Frederick Charles: pp. 28-29 left, 56 (Interior Design by Heather Faulding)

©Crandall & Crandall: pp. 25 (Interior Design by Pallette), 73 bottom (Interior Design by M. Joseph)

©Elizabeth Whiting Assoc's.: pp. 17 top, 54, 57, 62, ©Rodney Hyett: p. 38, 47, 78, 84, 89

©Phillip H. Ennis: pp. 65 bottom, 75, 98

Envision: ©Melabee Miller: pp. 20-21

©Feliciano: pp. 99

©Michael Garland: pp. 116-117 (Interior Design by Carla Schrad)

©Tria Giovan: pp. 12-13 (Design by Michael Foster), 36-37, 63-64 (Design by Charles Riley), 68 (Design by Charles Riley), 106 left-107, 110 left-111 (Design by Michael Foster), 119

©Philip Harvey, San Francisco (Interior Design by Osburn Design, San Francisco): pp. 42, 65 top

©Nancy Hill: pp. 10-11 (Interior Design by David Parker), 19 (Architecture by Robert Davis, AIA), 29 right, 30 (Courtesy of *House Beautiful*), 31 (Interior Design by Brassard Design Assoc.), 53 (Kitchens by Deane), 74 (Interior Design by Deborah Lipner, Ltd., Greenwich, CT)

©Houses and Interiors: pp. 17 bottom, 34-35, 73 top

Courtesy of IKEA: pp. 50 right, 80, 110 left, 112-113

The Interior Archive: ©Simon Brown: pp. 82-83

©Jim Kascoutas: pp. 43 both, 59, 81, 85

Courtesy of the Knoll Group: p.44 (Photography by Robert Kato); 70, 102 left

©Jennifer Levy: pp. 94 (Interior Design by Kieth Hone), 122

©Mark Lohman: pp. 49 bottom, 52, 100

©Richard Mandelkorn: pp. 77 bottom (Design by Celeste Cooper)

©Herman Miller, Inc.: pp. 118, ©Elliot Kaufman: pp. 51, 102 left-103, 115

©Peter Paige: p. 6

©Robert Perron: pp. 8-9, 50 left (Architecture by Knight), 26 left (Architecture by Lasar), 45 (Design by Amos)

©David Phelps: pp. 58 (Courtesy of *American Home Style* Magazine/ Architecture by James O'Connor), 77 top (Courtesy of *American Home Style* Magazine)

©Eric Roth: pp. 14 (Design by Anne Lenox-Partners in Design, Boston), 15, 16 (Design by Pomegranate Inn, Portland, ME), 24 (Design by Martin Potter-M.J. Berries, Boston), 40-41 (Architecture by Gary Wolf Architects, Inc., Boston), 69 bottom, 83 right, 86-87, 93 (Styling by Gwen Simpkins, Newton, MA), 97 (Design by Geib Truesdale Interior Design, Boston), 108-109 (Styling by Gwen Simpkins, Newton, MA), 120 (Design by Martin Potter-M.J. Berries, Boston), 123 (Design by Beverly Payeff, Brookline, NH)

©Bill Rothschild: pp. 69 top (Interior Design by Frank A. Lavin, Jr.), 72 (Interior Design by Patricia Bonis)

©Tim Street-Porter: pp. 71 (Interior Design by Frank Israel); 76 (Architecture/ Design by Brian Murphy), 92 top (Interior Design by Myra Hoefer)

Courtesy of Techline: pp. 95

©Brian Vanden Brink: pp. 2-3 (Architecture by Jefferson Riley, Center-brook Architects, CT), 26-27 top (Architecture by Dick Dudley, Concord, NH), 55 (Architecture by Chad Floyd, Centerbrook Architects, CT), 79, 92 bottom, 105 (Architecture by Jane Davis Doggett)

©Dominigue Vorillon: pp. 22-23 (Design by Goodman/Charlton), 46 (Design by Bernardo Urquieta), 66 (Design by Denise Domergue)

©Paul Warchol: pp. 39 (Design by Henry Smith-Miller+Laurie Hawkinson), 104 (Design by Weisz & Warchol Studio)

Jacket Design
Charles Donahue

Front Jacket Photography
(including Spine):
©Eric Roth (Styling by Gwen Simpkins, Newton, MA)

Back Jacket Photography:
©Brian Vanden Brink, (Design by Centerbrook Architects, CT)